DEPARTMENT OF HEALTH

Health and Personal Social Services Statistics for England

1999 edition

Editorial Team:	Lucinda Howe
	Peter Steele
	Grant Whiting

A publication of the Government Statistical Service

London: The Stationery Office

Applications for reproduction should be made in writing to the Copyright Unit, The Stationery Office, St. Clements House, 2-16 Colegate, Norwich NR3 1BQ

First Published 1999

ISBN 0 11 322306 4

Printed in the United Kingdom for The Stationery Office
J97467 C16 11/99 5673

CONTENTS

Introduction

Notes on Content

Section A – Public Health

Indicators of the Nation's Health
1.   Male expectation of life
2.   Female expectation of life
3.   Male deaths by selected causes
4.   Female deaths by selected causes
5.   Trends in adults general health, longstanding illness and acute sickness

Basic Population Data
6.   Mid-year resident population estimates, by age & regional office area

Health Related Behaviour
7.   Prevalence of smoking cigarettes among adults aged 16 and over
8.   Prevalence of smoking cigarettes among secondary school children aged 11 to 15 years
9.   Prevalence of alcohol consumption above 21/14 units a week
10.   Users presenting to drug misuse services for the first time

Morbidity
11.   Notification of selected infectious diseases
12.   HIV/AIDS and sexually transmitted diseases

Fertility
13.   Conceptions
14.   Deliveries and births
15.   Abortions to residents
16.   Contraception

Section B - Health Care

Primary and Community Care

General Dental Service
1.   Selected statistics
2.   Selected types of adult treatments

General Ophthalmic Services
3.   Selected statistics

Pharmaceutical Services
4.   Prescription items dispensed in the community
5.   Community pharmacies in contract with health authorities

CONTENTS

CONTENTS

The Department of Health is responsible for health services (such as GPs and hospitals) and Personal Social Services (such as residential care, child protection and home help) in England.

This publication contains a selection of statistics from across this range of services. It is intended both to provide a useful starting point into Department of Health statistics and act as a summary reference document. If you want to find out more detail about a particular topic a full list of the Department's statistical publications is included at the back. Each table also has the telephone number and email address of the relevant statistical contact.

This is the 26th publication of a series and an electronic version has also been developed which is available at www.doh.gov.uk/HPSSS/INDEX.HTM. This electronic version will be kept up to date through the year, as data become available.

Further statistical information is increasingly being made available at www.doh.gov.uk/public/stats1.htm.

This year I am seeking views on the how we produce and distribute this document. At the back of this document you will find a customer questionnaire and I would grateful if you could spare a few moments to photocopy and complete it before returning it to the address below. All comments will be gratefully received, as we are always looking to improve our statistical publications.

Peter Steele
HPSSS Editor
Statistics Division
Department of Health
Room 459C Skipton House
80 London Road
London SE1 6LH

Tel: 020 7972 5820
Fax: 020 7972 5660
Email: peter.steele@doh.gsi.gov.uk

NOTES ON CONTENT

Symbols and Conventions

The following symbols and abbreviations are used in the tables:

..	not available
-	nil or negligible
.	not applicable
ICD	International Classification of Diseases
DH	Department of Health
ONS	Office for National Statistics

In tables where figures have been rounded to the nearest final digit, there may be a slight discrepancy between the sum of the constituent items and the totals as shown.

Indicators of the Nation's Health

1. Male expectation of life
2. Female expectation of life
3. Male deaths by selected causes
4. Female deaths by selected causes
5. Trends in adults general health, longstanding illness and acute sickness

Basic Population Data

6. Mid-year resident population estimates, by age & regional office area

Health Related Behaviour

7. Prevalence of smoking cigarettes among adults aged 16 and over
8. Prevalence of smoking cigarettes among secondary school children aged 11 to 15 years
9. Prevalence of alcohol consumption above 21/14 units a week
10. Users presenting to drug misuse services for the first time

Morbidity

11. Notification of selected infectious diseases
12. HIV/AIDS and sexually transmitted diseases

Fertility

13. Conceptions
14. Deliveries and births
15. Abortions to residents
16. Contraception

Indicators of the Nation's Health: Male expectation of life at birth and from selected ages

England						Expectation of life (in years)
Age (in years)	1982	1992	1993	1994	1995	1996
At birth (0)	71.3	73.7	74.0	74.1	74.4	74.6
5	63.7	69.3	69.6	69.7	70.0	70.2
20	52.7	54.6	54.9	55.0	55.3	55.5
30	43.1	45.0	45.3	45.5	45.7	45.9
50	24.5	26.3	26.6	26.7	27.0	27.1
60	16.5	18.0	18.2	18.3	18.5	18.7
70	10.2	11.2	11.4	11.4	11.6	11.7
80	5.8	6.4	6.5	6.6	6.6	6.7

Source: Government Actuary's Department (GAD)

Contact: Steve Smallwood (GAD) 0207 211 2667
(email:steve.smallwood@gad.gov.uk)

See General Notes Section

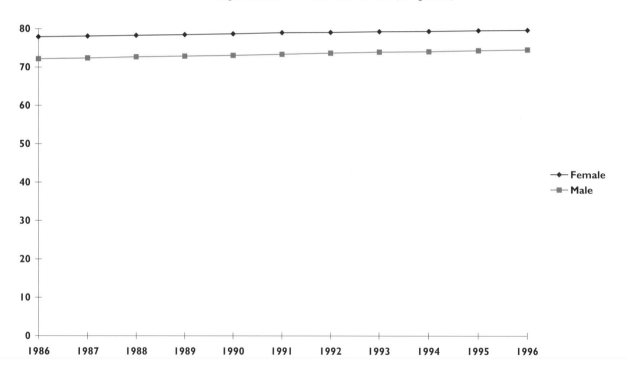

Expectation of life at birth (in years)

TABLE A2

Indicators of the Nation's Health: Female expectation of life at birth and from selected ages

England **Expectation of life (in years)**

Age (in years)	1982	1992	1993	1994	1995	1996
At birth (0)	77.3	79.1	79.3	79.4	79.6	79.7
5	73.1	74.6	74.9	74.9	75.1	75.2
20	58.3	59.8	60.0	60.1	60.3	60.3
30	48.5	50.0	50.2	50.3	50.5	50.5
50	29.6	30.9	31.1	31.2	31.4	31.4
60	21.0	22.1	22.3	22.4	22.5	22.6
70	13.5	14.5	14.6	14.6	14.7	14.7
80	7.6	8.4	8.5	8.5	8.6	8.6

Source: Government Actuary's Department (GAD)   *Contact: Steve Smallwood (GAD) 0207 211 2667*
                                                     (email: steve.smallwood@gad.gov.uk)

See General Notes Section

- Based on current mortality, womens expectation of life at birth would be 5 years longer than a man.
- The gap between men and womens life expectancy has been narrowing in recent years from 6 in 1982 to 5 in 1996.

Indicators of the Nation's Health: Male death rates by selected causes

England   **Rates per 100,000 population**

	1993	1994	1995	1996	1997	1998
All causes	**1,097.0**	**1,044.1**	**1,060.5**	**1,045.3**	**1,024.4**	**1,014.0**
All Malignant Neoplasms (ICD 140-208)	289.1	284.7	282.2	279.2	271.6	273.2
Stomach (ICD 151)	17.8	17.9	16.4	16.3	15.5	15.0
Colon, rectum, rectosigmoid junction & anus (ICD 153-4)	31.9	30.7	30.9	30.3	30.1	29.6
Pancreas (ICD 157)	11.2	10.9	10.8	11.0	10.8	10.9
Lung (ICD 162)	85.1	82.7	79.7	77.4	74.0	73.5
Prostate (ICD 185)	34.1	34.1	34.3	34.2	32.9	33.1
Diabetes mellitus (ICD 250)	11.2	10.7	11.1	11.0	10.5	10.6
All Circulatory diseases (ICD 390-459)	484.8	452.5	450.9	442.1	422.6	412.6
Ischaemic heart disease (ICD 410-14)	310.7	286.3	281.7	273.1	258.4	251.3
Cerebrovascular disease (ICD 430-8)	89.1	85.1	85.9	86.3	83.6	82.0
Pneumonia (ICD 480-6)	82.2	74.9	83.7	83.5	86.6	82.9
Bronchitis and allied conditions (ICD 490-6)	68.9	60.6	63.4	60.0	60.0	57.8
Chronic liver disease and cirrhosis (ICD 571)	6.6	7.3	8.3	8.6	9.6	10.7
All accidents and adverse effects (ICD E800-E949)	23.0	23.3	22.5	22.8	24.4	23.5
Road vehicle accidents (ICD E810-29)	9.6	9.1	8.6	8.9	9.4	8.9
Suicide (ICD E950-9, E980-9, excluding E988.8)	15.0	14.7	14.9	14.2	13.8	15.5

Source: Office for National Statistics (ONS)   *Contact: Allan Baker (ONS) 0207 533 5242*
                                               (email: allan.baker@ons.gov.uk)

See General Notes Section

Male deaths by selected causes, 1998

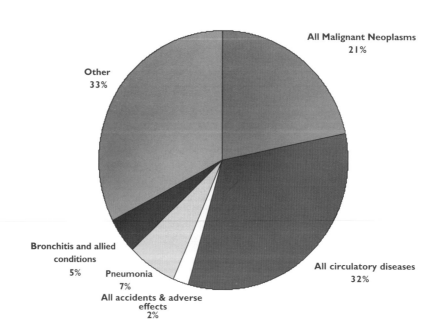

- Saving Lives - Our Healthier Nation has set targets to see real improvements by the year 2010. To reduce death rates from:
- cancers by at least a fifth in people under the age of 75;
- heart disease, stroke and related illnesses by at least two fifths in people aged under the age of 75;
- accidents by at least a fifth and the rates of serious injury by at least a tenth and suicide & undetermined injury by at least a fifth.

Indicators of the Nation's Health: Female death rates by selected causes

England					Rates per 100,000 population	
	1993	1994	1995	1996	1997	1998
All causes	**1,131.3**	**1,075.3**	**1,102.4**	**1,099.4**	**1,091.2**	**1,078.5**
All Malignant Neoplasms (ICD 140-208)	253.3	251.4	249.4	248.9	244.8	242.6
Stomach (ICD 151)	11.1	10.9	10.3	9.4	9.6	9.2
Colon, rectum, rectosigmoid junction & anus (ICD 153-4)	30.1	30.0	29.0	28.7	27.6	26.9
Pancreas (ICD 157)	11.5	11.4	11.5	11.4	11.2	11.1
Lung (ICD 162)	41.6	41.5	42.0	41.8	40.8	41.6
Breast (ICD 174)	49.3	48.2	47.2	45.9	45.0	43.8
Uterus (ICD 179-82)	10.5	9.8	9.9	9.9	9.4	9.1
Diabetes mellitus (ICD 250)	13.1	12.1	12.5	11.9	11.7	11.5
All circulatory diseases (ICD 390-459)	506.3	473.5	471.0	464.9	445.9	439.0
Ischaemic heart disease (ICD 410-14)	251.6	232.0	225.9	220.0	208.5	203.9
Cerebrovascular disease (ICD 430-8)	145.7	139.2	140.9	141.3	135.3	134.1
Pneumonia (ICD 480-6)	128.0	113.1	125.7	124.5	130.7	122.8
Bronchitis and allied conditions (ICD 490-6)	43.1	39.6	43.0	43.0	44.0	43.3
Chronic liver disease and cirrhosis (ICD 571)	4.8	5.0	5.4	5.7	6.2	6.3
All accidents & adverse effects (ICD E800-E949)	16.7	16.4	16.0	16.6	17.0	16.1
Road vehicle accidents (ICD E810-29)	4.0	3.8	3.7	3.5	3.4	3.3
Suicide (ICD E950-9, E980-9 excluding E988.8)	5.2	4.9	4.9	4.8	4.7	4.8

Source: Office for National Statistics (ONS)

Contact: Allan Baker (ONS) 0207 533 5242
(email: allan.baker@ons.gov.uk)

See General Notes Section

Female deaths by selected causes, 1998

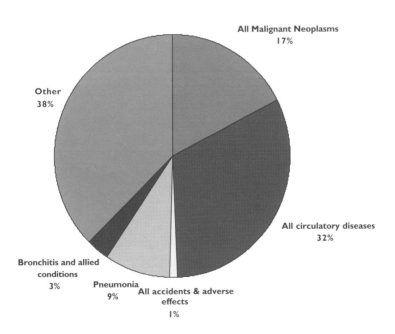

- Saving Lives - Our Healthier Nation has set targets to see real improvements by the year 2010. To reduce death rates from:
- cancers by at least a fifth in people under the age of 75;
- heart disease, stroke and related illnesses by at least two fifths in people aged under the age of 75;
- accidents by at least a fifth and the rates of serious injury by at least a tenth and suicide and undetermined injury by at least a fifth.

Indicators of the Nation's Health: Trends in adults general health, longstanding illness and acute sickness

England   Percentage

	1994	1995	1996	1997
Males				
Very good/good health	78	77	77	76
Very bad/bad health	5	5	6	6
At least one longstanding illness	39	42	43	44
Acute sickness	12	13	15	15
Females				
Very good/good health	75	76	75	73
Very bad/bad health	5	5	5	7
At least one longstanding illness	40	41	43	44
Acute sickness	15	17	19	19
Bases				
Males	7,176	7,332	7,485	3,895
Females	8,626	8,719	8,956	4,682
All adults	15,802	16,051	16,441	8,577

Source: Health Survey for England 1997   Contact: Michelle Marcelle 020 7972 5560
                                                        (email: michelle.marcelle@doh.gsi.gov.uk)

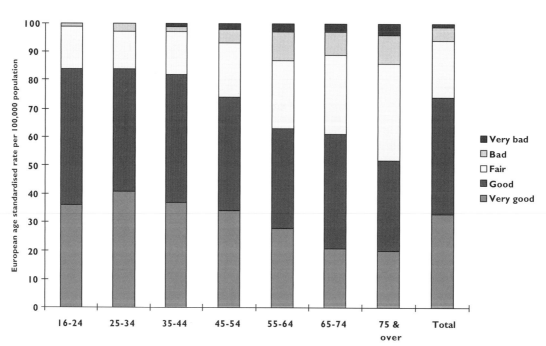

All adults self reported general health in 1997, by age

- In 1997, over 80% of adults aged 16-77 thought their health was good or very good.
- In 1997, 44% of adults reported having a longstanding illness.
- In 1997, 15% of men and 19% women reported having had acute sickness in two weeks preceding the interview.

Basic Population Data: Resident population estimates mid-year 1998, by age, persons & Department of Health Regional Office areas (as at 01/04/99)

England   **Thousands**

	All ages	Under 5	5-17	18-64	65-74	75 & over
England	**49,495**	**3,074**	**8,222**	**30,419**	**4,127**	**3,652**
Regional Office						
Northern and Yorkshire	6,339	381	1,075	3,870	554	458
Trent	5,134	307	850	3,145	450	381
West Midlands	5,333	335	916	3,246	457	379
North West	6,604	406	1,150	4,021	555	473
Eastern	5,377	333	880	3,302	458	404
London	7,187	505	1,146	4,614	480	442
South East	8,620	528	1,421	5,290	712	668
South West	4,901	279	784	2,931	461	446

Source: Office for National Statistics (ONS)   *Contact: Brett Leeming (ONS) 01329 813318*
(email: brett.leeming@ons.gov.uk)

• Nearly 16% of the population is aged 65 & over, while almost 23% is aged under 18.

Health Related Behaviour: Prevalence of smoking cigarettes among adults aged 16 and over by sex and age

England					Percentages
	1986	1990	1992	1994	1996
Males					
16-24	36	34	35	36	34
25-44	37	36	33	34	35
45-64	36	28	27	25	27
65 & over	25	22	19	16	15
Total	34	31	29	28	28
Females					
16-24	35	36	32	34	35
25-44	34	33	30	29	31
45-64	34	28	28	25	27
65 & over	18	16	17	14	16
Total	31	28	27	25	27

Source: ONS General Household Survey

Contact: Patsy Bailey 020 7972 5551
(email: patsy.bailey@doh.gsi.gov.uk)

See General Notes Section

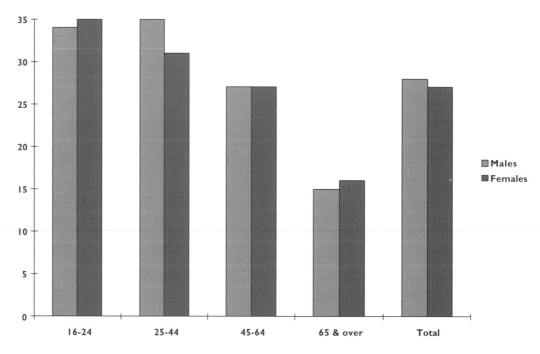

Prevalence of smoking cigarettes among adults aged 16 and over, 1996

- Cigarette smoking among adults aged 16 and over has declined markedly since 1986, from 34% to 28% among men, and from 31% to 27% among women.
- There was a small increase in cigarette smoking amongst women between 1994 and 1996, from 25% to 27%. It is not clear whether this increase is the beginning of a new trend, or whether it is a one off fluctuation.
- In 1996, smoking prevalence was highest among men aged 16-24 and 25-44, and among women aged 16-24.

Health Related Behaviour: Prevalence of smoking cigarettes among secondary school children aged 11 to 15 years by sex

England   **Percentages**

	1988	1990	1992	1994	1996	1998
Boys						
Regular smoker	7	9	9	10	11	9
Occasional smoker	5	6	6	9	8	8
Used to smoke	8	7	6	7	7	9
Tried smoking	23	22	22	21	22	20
Never smoked	58	56	57	53	53	54
Girls						
Regular smoker	9	11	10	13	15	12
Occasional smoker	5	6	7	10	10	8
Used to smoke	9	7	7	8	9	10
Tried smoking	19	18	19	17	18	18
Never smoked	59	58	57	52	48	51

Source: ONS Smoking, drinking and drug use among young teenagers in 1998.

Contact: Patsy Bailey 020 7972 5551 (email: patsy.bailey@doh.gsi.gov.uk)

See General Notes Section

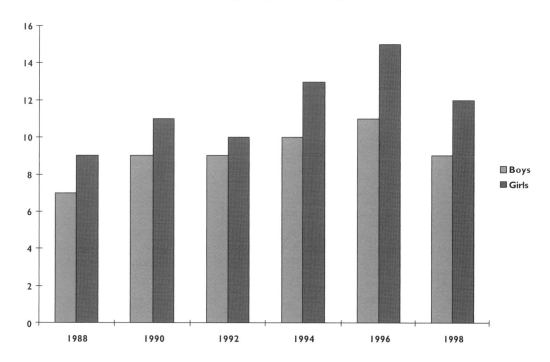

Prevalence of regular cigarette smoking by sex

- Prevalence of regular cigarette smoking increased between 1988 and 1996, but decreased in 1998. It is too early to say whether this is a temporary fluctuation or a reversal of the previous trend.
- Among those aged 11-15, girls are more likely to be regular smokers than boys (12% girls, 9% boys in 1998).
- The prevalence of cigarette smoking increases across the age range. In 1998, 1% of 11 year olds were regular smokers, compared to 24% of 15 year olds.

Health Related Behaviour: Prevalence of alcohol consumption above 21/14 units a week for men/women aged 18 and over

England   **Percentages**

	1986	1990	1992	1994	1996
Males (above 21 units)					
18-24	39	37	38	36	42
25-44	33	33	30	30	31
45-64	24	26	24	27	27
65 & over	13	14	15	17	18
Total	27	28	26	27	28
Females (above 14 units)					
18-24	19	18	19	20	22
25-44	13	13	14	16	16
45-64	8	10	12	13	14
65 & over	4	5	5	8	7
Total	10	11	12	13	14

Source: ONS General Household Survey   *Contact: Patsy Bailey 020 7972 5551 (email: patsy.bailey@doh.gsi.gov.uk)*
See General Notes Section

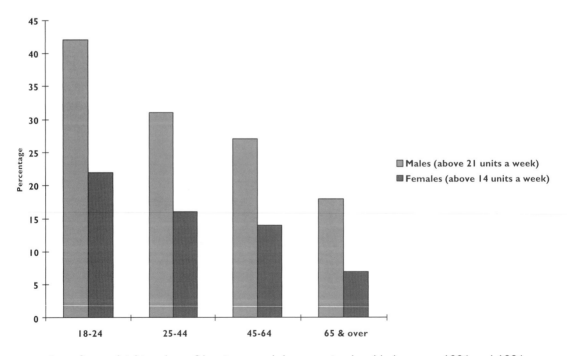

Alcohol consumption above 21/14 units a week by sex and age, 1996

- The proportion of men drinking above 21 units a week has remained stable between 1986 and 1996 at around 27%.
- The proportion of women drinking above 14 units a week has increased from 10% in 1986 to 14% in 1996.
- The proportion of adults drinking above these levels decreased with age.

Health Related Behaviour: Users presenting to drug misuse services for the first time

England   **Numbers**

Main drug		Six months ending			
	March 1994	Sept 1996	March 1997	Sept 1997	March 1998	Sept 1998
Total number of users	**17,864**	**24,879**	**25,925**	**21,996**	**23,916**	**28,599**
Heroin	8,546	14,334	15,597	12,392	13,635	16,081
Methadone	3,232	3,574	3,704	2,852	2,925	3,088
Other opiates	574	493	454	436	461	633
Amphetamines	1,786	2,248	2,009	1,999	2,141	2,490
Cannabis	1,205	1,533	1,660	1,934	2,201	2,775
Cocaine	714	870	1,020	925	1,143	1,663
Benzodiazepines	743	659	558	598	616	693
Ecstasy	175	268	246	223	141	196
Solvents	172	166	158	148	167	157
Other drugs	483	576	398	412	417	471
Not known	234	158	121	77	69	347

Source: DH Statistical Bulletin 1999/19   *Contact: Patsy Bailey 020 7972 5551 (email: patsy.bailey@doh.gsi.gov.uk)*
See General Notes Section

Users presenting to drug misuse services for first time, by age group. Six months to Sept 98

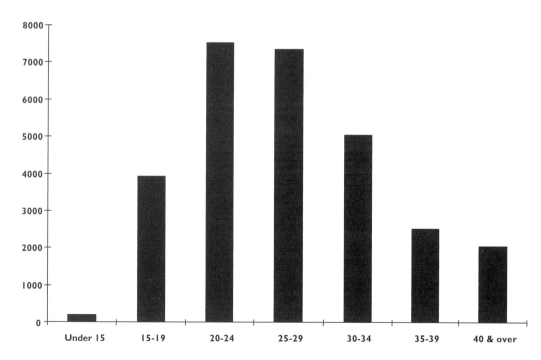

- During the six month period ending September 1998, the number of users presenting to drug misuse agencies, and reported to Regional Drug Misuse Databases increased by 20% over the previous 6 month period.
- Part of this increase is likely to be due to change in reporting practice.
- About three times as many men as women presented to drug misuse services.
- In the six months ending September 1998, the most commonly used "main drug" was heroin (used by 56%), followed by methadone (11%), cannabis (10%) and amphetamines (9%).

Morbidity: Notification of selected infectious diseases

England						Numbers
	1988	1994	1995	1996	1997	1998
Dysentery	3,601	6,690	4,373	2,256	2,236	1,767
Food poisoning						
total	37,754	75,666	75,499	77,557	87,740	87,971
formally notified	26,198	45,022	45,560	46,574	50,105	49,939
otherwise ascertained	11,556	30,644	29,939	30,983	37,635	38,032
Tuberculosis	4,960	5,409	5,426	5,493	5,664	5,915
Whooping cough	4,803	3,680	1,757	2,252	2,827	1,471
Scarlet fever	5,817	6,005	5,138	4,769	3,466	3,239
Meningitis	2,774	1,614	2,062	2,477	2,144	1,925
of which meningococcal meningitis	1,202	827	1,026	1,056	1,116	1,080
Meningococcal septicaemia	..	390	654	1,027	1,300	1,342
Viral hepatitis	4,868	3,443	3,156	2,240	3,003	2,981
Malaria	1,245	1,119	1,286	1,641	1,459	1,098
Measles	80,138	14,734	6,931	5,297	3,634	3,524
Mumps	..	2,380	1,852	1,678	1,840	1,519
Rubella	..	6,079	5,936	8,420	3,120	3,089

Source: Communicable Disease Surveillance Centre (CDSC)   *Contact: Douglas Harding (CDSC) 0208 200 6868 ext. 4549*
(email: dharding@phls.nhs.uk)

See General Notes Section

Morbidity: HIV/AIDS and sexually transmitted diseases

England						Percentages and numbers	
	1987	1993	1994	1995	1996	1997	1998
HIV cases diagnosed (number)	**1,917**	**2,143**	**2,138**	**2,232**	**2,238**	**2,215**	**2,275**
Exposure category (percentage)							
homosexual intercourse	73	59	58	57	59	53	48
heterosexual intercourse	9	30	31	32	29	35	39
injecting drug use	12	6	6	6	6	5	4
blood products	2	1	1	1	1	1	0.3
AIDS cases diagnosed (number)	**640**	**1,623**	**1,686**	**1,577**	**1,287**	**937**	**581**
Sexually Transmitted Diseases (STDs), new cases (thousands)							
all STDs except HIV/AIDS	..	354.0	381.2	398.0	424.3	455.5	..
syphilis	2.4	1.3	1.4	1.4	1.2	1.3	..
gonorrhoea	46.3	12.0	11.8	12.1	14.4	15.4	..
chlamydia	..	34.0	36.8	38.8	44.7	54.4	..
herpes	18.9	25.5	26.8	26.7	27.6	27.4	..
wart virus	52.2	84.7	86.7	92.0	97.8	106.0	..

Source: CDSC (HIV/AIDS) KC60 (STDs)   *Contact: Lesz Lancucki 020 7972 5533 (email: lesz.lancucki@doh.gsi.gov.uk)*
See General Notes Section

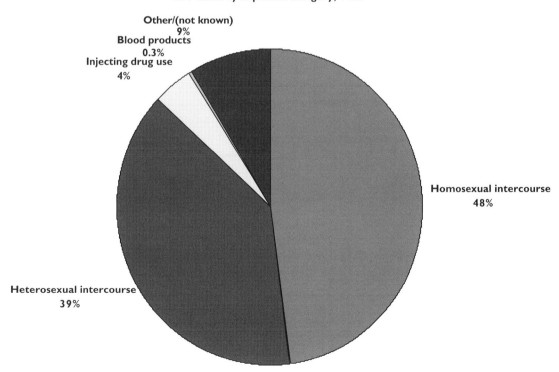

HIV cases by exposure category, 1996

- New cases of all sexually transmitted diseases, except herpes, rose in 1997.
- Percentage of new HIV cases thought to have been acquired though heterosexual intercourse was about 30% from 1992 to 1996, but has since risen to 39%.

Fertility: Conceptions

England   Numbers and percentages

	1991	1992	1993	1994	1995	1996	1997
Conceptions (thousands)							
all ages	809.1	784.9	776.8	760.4	749.9	774.5	759.5
under 20	96.9	87.7	81.7	80.0	81.1	88.8	89.9
under 16	7.4	6.7	6.8	7.3	7.5	8.2	7.7
Rate per 1,000 females							
all ages	77.8	76.4	76.3	74.8	73.8	76.1	74.5
under 20	64.8	61.7	59.6	58.6	58.5	62.9	62.2
under 16	9.3	8.3	8.0	8.3	8.5	9.3	8.8
Percentage terminated by abortion							
all ages	19.5	19.5	19.3	19.6	19.9	21.0	21.5
under 20	34.8	34.2	34.6	35.1	35.1	36.7	37.2
under 16	51.1	48.8	50.4	50.6	48.0	49.6	50.1

Source: ONS   *Contact: Lesz Lancucki 020 7972 5533 (email: lesz.lancucki@doh.gsi.gov.uk)*
See General Notes Section

Under 16 conception rates per 1,000 females

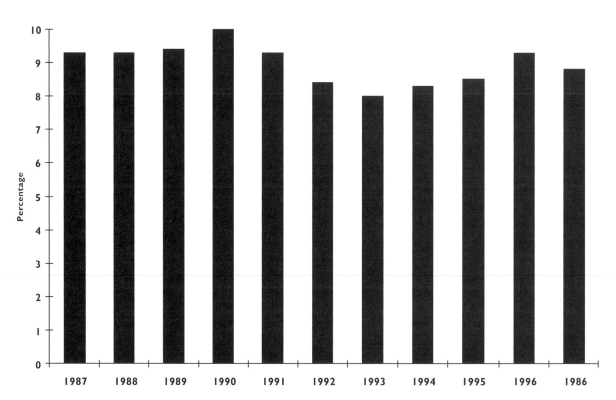

- Reducing under-age conception rates was a Health of the Nation target; although rates fell from a peak in 1990 to 8.0 per 1,000 females in 1993, they have since increased.

TABLE A14

Fertility: Deliveries and births

England **Numbers and percentages**

	1992	1993	1994	1995	1996	1997	1998
Deliveries							
Number (thousands)	646.6	631.7	624.0	607.8	608.8	601.5	..
Percentage occuring at home	1.3	1.6	1.8	1.9	2.1	2.3	..
Estimated percentage by caesarean section	13.8	15.0	15.5	15.8	16 (p)	17 (p)	..
Births							
Total births (thousands)	651.8	636.5	629.0	613.3	614.2	608.6	602.5
Stillbirths (thousands)	2.8	3.6	3.6	3.4	3.3	3.3	3.2
Perinatal mortality rate (per 1,000)	7.6	8.9	8.8	8.8	8.7	8.3	8.2 (p)
Infant mortality rate (per 1,000)	6.5	6.3	6.1	6.1	6.1	5.9	5.6 (p)
Community maternity care							
Antenatal contacts per maternity	5.5	6.3	6.8	7.1	7.5	7.7	7.6
Postnatal contacts per maternity	8.7	8.7	8.7	8.4	8.4	8.1	7.7

Source: ONS, HES, Form KC54. (p) = provisional.
See General Notes Section

Contact: Lesz Lancucki 020 7972 5533
(email: lesz.lancucki@doh.gsi.gov.uk)

Percentage of deliveries by caesarean section

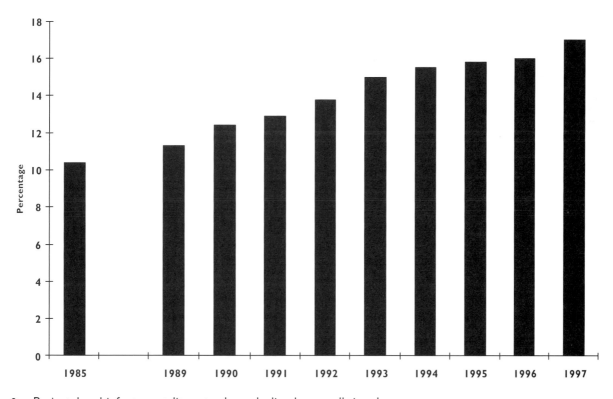

• Perinatal and infant mortality rates have declined to an all time low.

Fertility: Abortions to residents

England							Numbers and percentages
	1986	1993	1994	1995	1996	1997	1998
Number (thousands)	**140.9**	**150.9**	**149.7**	**147.9**	**160.6**	**162.8**	**169.6**
Gestation (weeks)(percentage)							
under 9	33.9	39.6	40.8	42.3	40.3	41.5	41.5
9-12	53.4	49.4	48.1	47.0	48.4	47.7	47.5
13-19	11.3	9.8	9.8	9.5	10.0	9.6	9.6
20 & over	1.4	1.2	1.2	1.2	1.3	1.2	1.3
Statutory grounds (percentage)							
A (alone or with B, C or D)	..	0.1	0.1	0.1	0.1	0.1	0.1
B (alone or with C or D)	..	2.5	2.1	1.6	1.5	1.2	1.2
C (alone)	..	86.9	87.7	88.8	90.2	91.1	91.4
D (alone or with C)	..	9.3	9.0	8.3	7.1	6.5	6.4
E (alone or with A, B, C or D)	..	1.2	1.1	1.2	1.2	1.1	1.1
F or G	..	0.0	0.0	0.0	0.0	0.0	0.0
Percentage purchased by NHS	**49.8**	**62.4**	**66.8**	**70.3**	**71.9**	**72.2**	**73.5**

Source: ONS
See General Notes Section

Contact: Lesz Lancucki 020 7972 5533 (email: lesz.lancucki@doh.gsi.gov.uk)

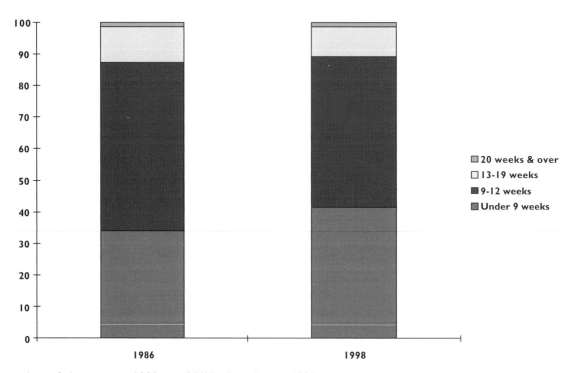

Percentage of abortions by gestation

Legend:
- 20 weeks & over
- 13-19 weeks
- 9-12 weeks
- Under 9 weeks

- The number of abortions in 1998 was 20% higher than in 1986.
- Over 40% of abortions in 1998 were at under 9 weeks gestation, compared with nearly 34% in 1986.
- Nearly 74% of abortions in 1998 were purchased by NHS, compared with about 50% in the period 1986 to 1991.

Fertility: Contraception

England   Numbers and percentages

	1992-93	1993-94	1994-95	1995-96	1996-97	1997-98	1998-99
Survey data (females aged 16-49)							
using pill (%)	..	25	..	25	..	26	..
using condom (%)	..	17	..	18	..	21	..
self or partner sterilised (%)	..	24	..	24	..	21	..
not using contraception (%)	..	28	..	27	..	26	..
Family Planning Clinic Activity							
Females seen (thousands)	1,081	1,095	1,129	1,160	1,182	1,191	1,179
Females seen (rate per 100 population)							
total all ages	10.5	10.8	11.1	11.4	11.6	11.7	11.6
under 16	3.8	4.9	6.4	7.2	7.4	7.6	7.4
16-19	15.2	16.8	18.8	20.3	21.5	22.2	22.1
20-24	14.2	14.5	15.2	16.2	16.9	17.5	18.3
25-34	9.9	9.7	9.3	9.5	9.5	9.4	9.2
35 & over	7.4	7.5	7.9	7.6	7.4	7.4	7.0
Emergency contraception prescribed: occasions (thousands)	70.4	85.0	104.6	149.3	198.7	210.2	217.5
GP activity							
Women registered for contraceptives (thousands)	3,309.8	3,421.4	3,374.7	3,578.0	3,603.4	3,808.3	..

Source: GHS and Form KT31
See General Notes Section   *Contact: Lesz Lancucki 020 7972 5533 (email: lesz.lancucki@doh.gsi.gov.uk)*

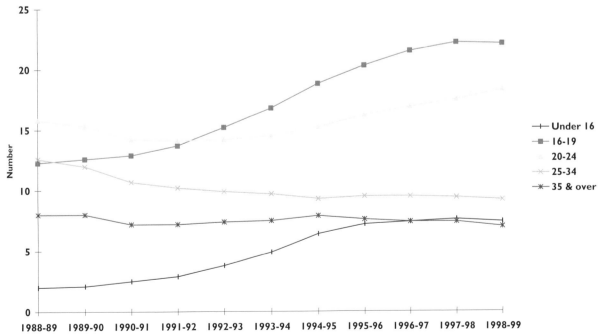

Percentage of female population attending family planning clinics by age

- Nationally, more women aged 16-49 reported the use of a condom for contraception in 1997 (21%) than ten years earlier (13%).
- About 1 in 13 women aged under 16 and 1 in 5 women aged 16-19 sought advice on contraception in 1997-98 from family planning clinics.

Primary and Community Care

General Dental Service

1. Selected statistics
2. Selected types of adult treatments

General Ophthalmic Services

3. Selected statistics

Pharmaceutical Services

4. Prescription items dispensed in the community
5. Community pharmacies in contract with health authorities

Community Health and Prevention

6. Community and cross sector services
7. Community and cross sector services (continued)
8. Cancer screening
9. Vaccination and immunisation
10. Community Dental Service activity

Hospitals

Hospital Inpatient Activity

11. Finished consultant episodes by sector; NHS trusts
12. Finished consultant episodes by selected diagnostic group
13. Finished consultant episodes by major diagnostic group
14. Finished consultant episodes, all specialities
15. Finished consultant episodes, the most frequently performed operative procedures
16. Average daily number of available beds by sector; NHS trusts
17. Waiting Lists - Patients waiting for elective admission, by speciality

Hospital Outpatient Activity

18. Outpatient attendances by sector, NHS trusts
19. Waiting Times - Patients seen following GP written referral, and time waited from referral to consultation

Patient's Charter

20. Performance against key standards

Mental Health & Learning Disability

21. Hospital and community occupied bed days commissioned for people with a mental illness
22. Hospital beds & places in residential & nursing care homes for people with learning disabilities
23. Hospital beds & places in residential & nursing care homes for people with mental illness
24. Admissions to NHS hospitals under a learning disability specialty
25. Admissions to NHS hospitals under mental illness specialties
26. Other NHS activity

General Dental Service: Selected statistics

England

	1988-89	1993-94	1994-95	1995-96	1996-97	1997-98	1998-99
Number of dentists (1)							
Total	15,070	15,773	15,885	15,951	16,336	16,728	17,245
of which principals (2)	14,840	15,143	15,084	15,064	15,280	15,509	15,820
Number of patients registered (3) **(thousands)**							
Adults (4)	..	21,530	21,050	19,994	19,524	19,383	16,721
Children (5)	..	7,396	7,367	7,292	7,270	7,367	6,775
Number of courses of treatment (thousands)							
Adults	24,027	24,848	24,913	24,752	24,580	25,268	26,171
Expenditure (6) **(£ millions)**							
Gross expenditure	949.7	1,221.7	1,279.4	1,289.5	1,323.1	1,347.6	1,437.7
Paid by patients	290.6	367.0	383.3	381.2	383.0	388.4	419.6
Paid out of public funds	659.1	854.7	896.1	908.4	940.1	959.1	1,018.1

See General Notes Section

Contact: Sharon Lea 020 7972 5392 (email: sharon.lea@doh.gsi.gov.uk)

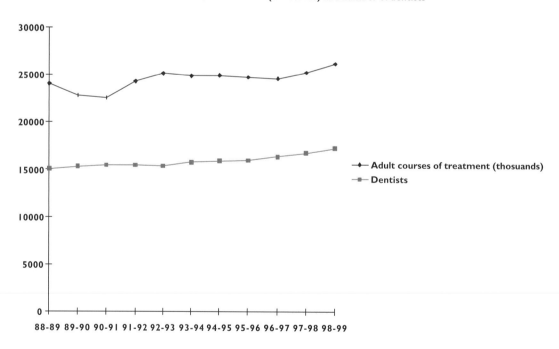

Number of adult courses of treatment (thousands) and number of dentists

- The number of dentists in the General Dental Service increased by 1,472 (9.3%) in the five years to September 1998. Principals increased by 677 whilst assistants rose by 639 from 223 to 862.
- Registration numbers have fallen in 1998-99 because of the change in the registration period (see General Notes section).
- The number of adult courses of treatment remained stable between 1993-94 and 1996-97 increasing in 1997-98 and 1998-99. Public funds met 71% of expenditure in 1998-99 compared to 70% in 1993-94.
- More than 25% of adult courses of treatment are delivered free or at a reduced charge. All dental treatment for children is free.

General Dental Service: Selected types of adult treatments

England   **Thousands**

	1988-89	1993-94	1994-95	1995-96	1996-97	1997-98	1998-99
Examination and report							
Number	20,904	19,488	19,328	19,226	18,946	19,512	20,161
Cost (£)	90,996	94,192	98,752	100,611	102,561	109,405	120,269
Periodontal Treatment (£)	92,821	122,014	127,557	130,706	134,624	143,142	153,792
Fillings (£)	175,270	163,773	165,026	163,427	164,080	170,465	177,259
Root Fillings (£)	37,356	37,861	38,929	39,258	39,103	38,818	41,512
Inlays and crowns (£)	154,177	139,731	148,911	145,925	140,790	113,761	123,189
Bridges (£)	30,997	29,455	30,697	27,528	24,125	21,129	24,181
Dentures and repairs to dentures (£)	122,904	104,000	107,232	104,283	102,585	103,393	108,052
All adult treatments (£)	764,593	793,442	826,230	823,338	825,272	821,697	877,609

Contact: Sharon Lea 020 7972 5392 (email: sharon.lea@doh.gsi.gov.uk)

See General Notes Section

Selected adult treatment costs as a percentage of all adult treatment costs

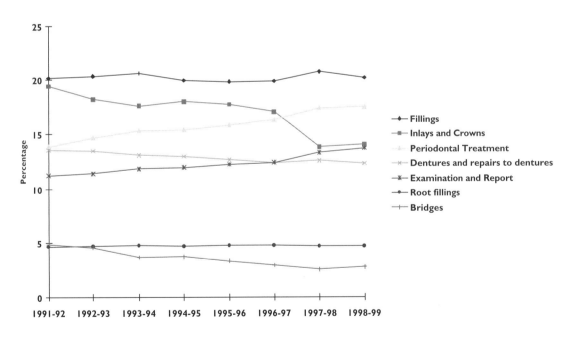

- The number of examination and reports was stable between 1993-94 and 1996-97 but increased in 1997-98 and 1998-99.
- The cost of advanced treatments fell between 1995-96 and 1997-98 despite increases in fees but increased in 1998-99.
- Crowns figures may be affected by a rationalisation of the crowns section of the feescale introduced in December 1996.
- The changing pattern of GDS treatments may partly reflect changes in the amounts of treatments being carried out privately.

General Ophthalmic Services: Selected statistics

England   Number

	1990-91	1993-94	1994-95	1995-96	1996-97	1997-98	1998-99
Number of practitioners							
Ophthalmic medical practitioners	779	705	650	658	675	696	733
Optometrists	5,652	5,914	5,972	6,120	6,264	6,395	6,572
Number of GOS sight tests (thousands)							
GOS sight tests: Total	**4,154**	**5,935**	**6,383**	**6,512**	**6,808**	**6,991**	**6,992**
By ophthalmic medical practitioners	405	489	480	453	470	474	426
By optometrists	3,748	5,446	5,903	6,058	6,338	6,517	6,566
Number of vouchers reimbursed (thousands)	**2,432**	**3,485**	**3,741**	**3,815**	**3,967**	**3,935**	**3,777**

Contact: Helen Dixon: 020 7972 5507 (email: helen.dixon@doh.gsi.gov.uk)

See General Notes Section

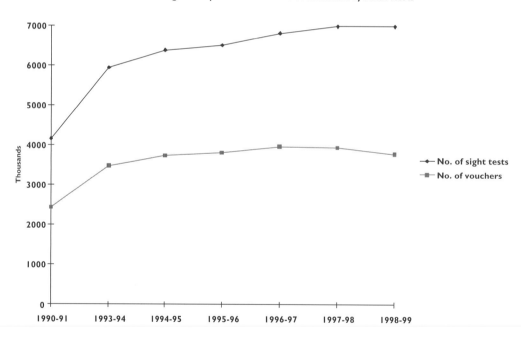

Numbers of GOS sight tests paid for and vouchers reimbursed by HAs/FHSAs

- The number of ophthalmic practitioners has been increasing for some years. 7,305 ophthalmic practitioners held contracts with at least one Health Authority to carry out NHS sight tests in England at 31 December 1998, an increase of 3% on 1997.
- The number of NHS sight tests paid for by Health Authorities (previously Family Health Service Authorities) has increased steadily since 1990-91.
- In 1998-99, Health Authorities in England paid for 6.99 million NHS sight tests, the same as in 1997-98 and an increase of 68% on 1990-91.
- In 1998-99, 3.8 million vouchers were reimbursed, a decrease of 4% on 1997-98 and an increase of 55% on 1990-91. The number of vouchers reimbursed by HAs (previously FHSAs) increased between the first full year of the scheme (1987-88) and 1996-97.

Pharmaceutical Services: Prescription items dispensed in the community

England

	Unit	1994	1995	1996	1997	1998
All prescriptions						
Number of prescription items	Millions	456.0	473.3	484.9	500.2	513.2
NIC of prescription items	£ millions	3,403.8	3,680.6	4,007.0	4,367.5	4,701.5
Average NIC of prescription items	£s	7.47	7.78	8.26	8.73	9.16
Average prescription items per head	Number	9.4	9.7	9.9	10.1	10.4
Average NIC per head	£s	69.90	75.27	81.68	88.63	95.09
Prescription items dispensed generically	Per cent	41	43	45	47	48
Prescription items prescribed generically	Per cent	52	55	58	60	63
NIC of items dispensed generically	Per cent	12	13	13	15	16
NIC of items prescribed generically	Per cent	37	42	44	47	50
Exempt prescriptions						
Number of prescription items	Millions	342.4	360.8	377.6	388.2	399.1
NIC of prescription items	£ millions	2,409.9	2,635.9	2,940.8	3,191.1	3,445.1
Average NIC per prescription item	£s	7.04	7.31	7.79	8.22	8.63
Exempt prescription items of total	Per cent	82.7	83.8	85.6	85.4	85.4

Source: Statistics of prescriptions dispensed in the
community - England 1988 to 1998
See General Notes Section

Contact: Jim Rodger 020 7972 5515
(email: jim.rodger@doh.gsi.gov.uk)

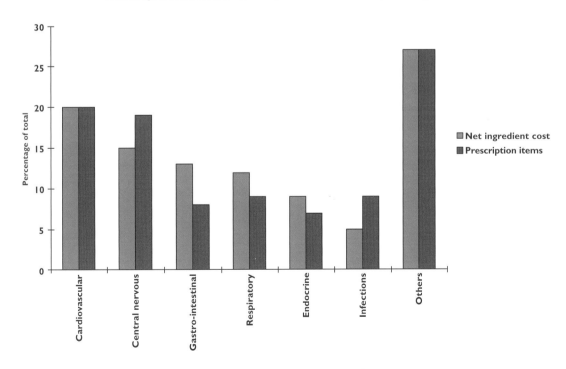

Percentage breakdown of all items dispensed and their NIC by BNF chapters

- 513 million prescription items were dispensed in 1998, an increase of 13% from 1994.
- The net ingredient cost of all prescription items in 1998 was £4,701 million, an increase of 38% or 24% in real terms over 1994.
- 48% of prescription items dispensed were dispensed generically in 1998, compared to 41% in 1994.
- 85% of prescription items dispensed by community pharmacists and appliance contractors were exempt or free of charge, compared to 83% in 1994.

Pharmaceutical Services: Community pharmacies in contract with health authorities at 31 March

England   **Number**

	1992-93	1993-94	1994-95	1995-96	1996-97	1997-98	1998-99
Number of contracting pharmacies	9,763	9,766	9,771	9,787	9,775	9,785	9,782

Source: Prescription Pricing Authority   *Contact: Marjorie Wilson 020 7972 5502 (email: marjorie.wilson@doh.gsi.gov.uk)*
See General Notes Section

- There was little change between 1992-93 and 1998-99 in the number of pharmacies in contract to dispense National Health Service prescriptions.

Community Health and Prevention: Community and cross sector services

England							Numbers and percentages
	1992-93	1993-94	1994-95	1995-96	1996-97	1997-98	1998-99
District Nursing							
New patients (thousands)	2,153	2,210	2,285	2,344	2,336	2,245	2,315
Average contacts per new patient	17	17	17	16	16	16	15
Health Visiting							
Clients seen (thousands)	3,669	3,717	3,711	3,713	3,697	3,631	3,563
Chiropody							
New clients (thousands)	966	1,006	975	951	975	936	896
Average contacts per new client	8	8	9	9	9	9	9
Speech and Language Therapy							
New clients (thousands)	270	285	297	296	316	330	327
Percentage referred from community	70	69	66	64	64	63	62

Source KC56,KC55,KT23,KT29.   *Contact: Lesz Lancucki   020 7972 5533 (email: lesz.lancucki@doh.gsi.gov.uk)*
See General Notes Section

Community Health and Prevention: Community and cross sector services (continued)

England   Numbers and percentages

	1992-93	1993-94	1994-95	1995-96	1996-97	1997-98	1998-99
Occupational Therapy							
New clients (thousands)	883	945	1,018	1,102	1,135	1,153	1,156
Percentage referred from community	22	21	21	22	23	22	23
Physiotherapy							
New clients (thousands)	3,363	3,530	3,904	4,056	4,070	4,141	4,177
Percentage referred from community	30	31	32	31	34	34	35
Ambulance Service							
Emergency calls (thousands)	2,250	2,411	2,610	2,856	2,994	3,161	3,291
Percentage responded to within							
14 minutes (urban) or 19 minutes (rural)	88.0	89.0	89.8	91.4	94.7	94.4	92.8

Source: KT26, KT27, KA34
See General Notes Section

Contact: Lesz Lancucki 020 7972 5533 (email: lesz.lancucki@doh.gsi.gov.uk)

Ambulance service emergency call response times, England 1992-93 to 1998-99

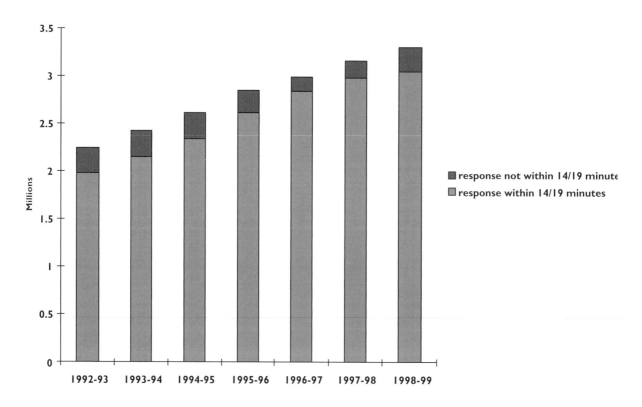

- In 1998-99, 92.8% of ambulance emergency calls received a response within 14 minutes (in urban areas) or 19 minutes (in rural areas) compared with 88% in 1992-93.

TABLE B8

Community Health and Prevention: Cancer screening

England | | | | | | Numbers and percentages |
|---|---|---|---|---|---|---|---|
| | 1992-93 | 1993-94 | 1994-95 | 1995-96 | 1996-97 | 1997-98 | 1998-99 |
| **Cervical screening programme** | | | | | | | |
| Coverage at end of year (percentage of target population) | 86 | 87 | 84 | 84 | 84 | 84 | 84 |
| women screened - all ages (thousands) | .. | .. | 3,756 | 3,771 | 3,639 | 3,756 | 3,647 |
| percentage with non-negative test results - all ages (1) | 5.1 | 5.1 | 5.6 | 5.6 | 5.7 | 7.8 | 7.9 |
| **Breast screening programme** | | | | | | | |
| Coverage at end of year (percentage of target population) | .. | .. | 64 | 65 | 66 | 66 | .. |
| Women screened - aged 50-64 (thousands) | 945 | 961 | 976 | 976 | 1,007 | 1,060 | .. |
| Cancer detected per 1,000 women screened - aged 50-64 | 5.7 | 5.1 | 5.0 | 5.0 | 5.3 | 5.6 | .. |

(1) 1992-93 to 1996-97 non-negative test result
figures were most recent test result. 1997-98 based on most severe result.
See General Notes Section

Contact: Lesz Lancucki 020 7972 5533
(email: lesz.lancucki@doh.gsi.gov.uk)

Community Health and Prevention: Vaccination and immunisation

England							Numbers and percentages
	1992-93	1993-94	1994-95	1995-96	1996-97	1997-98	1998-99
Percentage of children immunised by their 2nd birthday							
Diphtheria/tetanus/polio	95	95	95	96	96	96	95
Pertussis (whooping cough)	92	93	93	94	94	94	94
Measles/mumps/rubella	92	91	91	92	92	91	88
Haemophilus influenzae b	..	75	91	94	95	95	95
BCG vaccinations by age (thousands)							
under 1	44	47	53	56	64	65	68
1-9	4	6	5	6	6	6	5
10-15	346	409	256	509	407	442	395
16 & over	6	6	4	5	6	5	7

Source: Form KC50, KC51, COVER   *Contact: Lesz Lancucki 020 7972 5533 (email: lesz.lancucki@doh.gsi.gov.uk)*

See General Notes Section

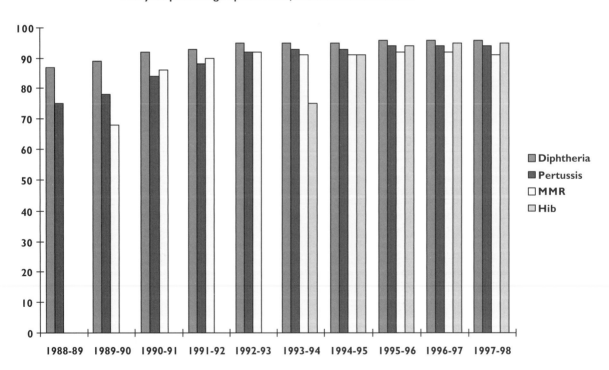

Two year percentage uptake rates, selected immunisations

- The proportion of children who have been immunised by their second birthday against diphtheria, tetanus and polio rose in 1995-96 to 96%, the highest ever recorded.
- Uptake of immunisation against pertussis and of immunisation against haemophilus influenzae b reached 95% in 1996-97.

Community Health and Prevention: Community Dental Service activity

England

	1991-92	1992-93	1993-94	1994-95	1995-96	1996-97	1997-98
Community Dental Staff (whole-time equivalent)							
Total	1,135	1,094	1,079	1,029	1,037	1,054	1,060
Dental Officers : Administrative	115	118	101	99	110	103	97
Clinical	1,020	976	978	930	927	951	964
All Patient Contacts (thousands)							
Screening programmes : Patient contacts(1)(2)	3,281	3,206	3,168	3,190	3,114	2,997	3,050
of which referred for treatment	805	783	740	739	724	638	608
Dental Education : Patient contacts (1)(2)(3)	1,443	1,550	1,524	1,667	1,722	1,841	n/a
Number of programmes	33	35	37	43	41	42	51
Patient Care (thousands)							
Patient contacts in year (4)(5)	1,265	1,263	1,223	1,211	1,153	1,132	1,096
Children under 4 years	148	148	140	140	132	123	114
Children 5 to 15 years	973	955	921	897	837	814	777
Adults 16 to 64 years	113	119	126	135	140	148	158
Adults 65 & over	31	33	36	39	44	46	48

Contact: Sharon Lea 020 7972 5392 (email: sharon.lea@doh.gsi.gov.uk)

See General Notes Section

Episodes of care containing some treatment items

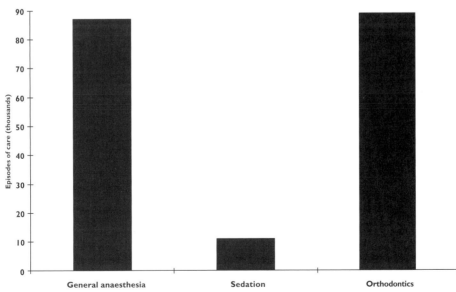

- During the period 1991-92 to 1996-97 the total number of patient contacts in screening programmes has gradually fallen to 3.0 million. There has been a slight increase in 1997-98 to 3.1 million.
- The number of initial patient contacts was 1.1 million in 1997-98, a decrease of about 0.2 million on 1991-92.
- The number of dental staff fell by 106 whole-time equivalent between 1991-92 and 1994-95, but increased by 31 whole-time equivalent between 1994-95 and 1997-98.

Hospital Inpatient Activity: Finished consultant episodes by sector; NHS trusts

England							Thousands
Sector	1987-88	1992-93	1993-94	1994-95	1995-96	1996-97	1997-98
All specialties	**8,245**	**9,635**	**10,095**	**10,540**	**11,037**	**11,275**	**11,530**
Acute	..	7,242	7,650	8,096	8,519	8,710	9,016
Geriatric	..	530	558	554	563	554	534
Mental illness	..	234	237	239	243	241	236
Learning disabilities	..	56	55	53	56	56	58
Maternity	..	964	994	1,006	1,082	1,143	1,129
All well babies	587	609	602	592	574	572	557

Source: KP70 return　　　　　　Contact: Mohamed Adrish 0113 2545235 (email: mohamed.adrish@doh.gsi.gov.uk)
See General Notes Section

Finished consultant episodes; NHS trusts

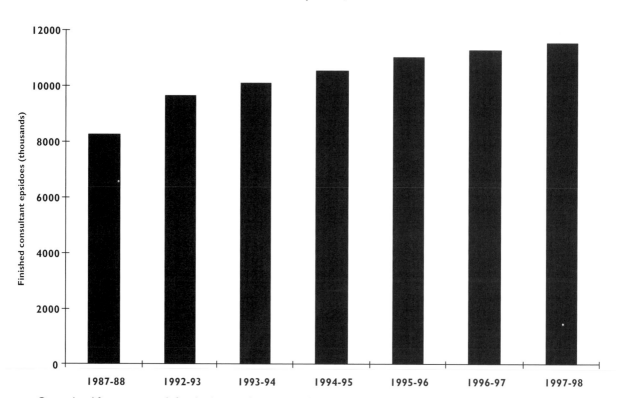

- Over the 10 year period, finished consultant episodes have been increased by an average 3.4% per annum.

Hospital Inpatient Activity: Finished consultant episodes by selected diagnostic group and age, year ending 31 March 1998

England: NHS hospitals   **Thousands**

Main diagnosis	ICD 10 codes	All ages	Under 15	15-44	45-64	65-74	75 & over
All diagnoses	**A00 - Z99**	**11,438**	**1,667**	**3,684**	**2,360**	**1,581**	**2,132**
Neoplasm	C00 - D48	1,190	43	188	419	291	249
Mental disorder	F00 - F99	231	16	110	43	20	41
Nervous system	G00 - G99	215	20	55	60	31	49
Circulatory system	I00 - I99	1,007	7	88	298	265	349
Respiratory System	J00 - J99	687	198	129	103	99	157
Digestive system	K00 - K93	1,180	116	334	321	189	221
Genito-urinary system	N00 - N99	763	47	295	214	100	107
Pregnancy etc.	O00 - O99	1,147	1	1,124	1	0	12
Injury & poisoning	S00 - T99	736	132	282	107	62	152
Other (not mentioned above)		4,282	1,086	1,080	793	526	793

Source: Hospital Episode Statistics   *Contact: Steve Price 020 7972 5683 (email: stephen.price@doh.gsi.gov.uk)*
See General Notes Section

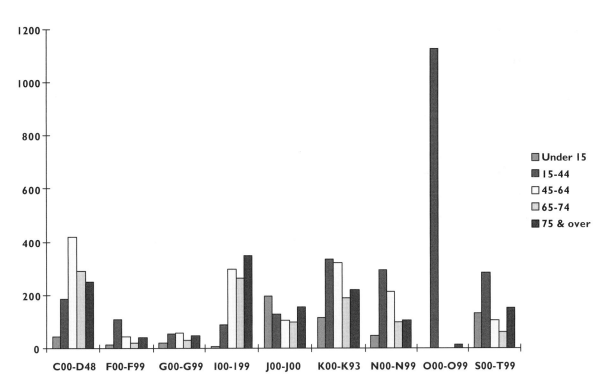

Finished consultant episodes, by selected diagnostic group and age

- ICD 10 codes replaced ICD 9 codes in 1995-96 (consequently these figures are not directly comparable with those from earlier years).

Hospital Inpatient Activity: Finished consultant episodes by major diagnostic group

England: NHS hospitals   **Thousands**

Main diagnosis	ICD 10 codes	1994-95	1995-96	1996-97	1997-98
All diagnoses	**A00 - Z99**	**9,475**	**11,042**	**11,359**	**11,438**
Infectious & parasitic diseases	A00 - B99	124	134	129	133
Neoplasms	C00 - D48	904	1,032	1,079	1,190
Diseases of blood and blood forming organs	D50 - D89	133	126	134	143
Endocrine, nutritional and metabolic	E00 - E90	135	126	128	135
Mental disorder	F00 - F99	318	289	245	231
Diseases of the nervous system, eye and ear	G00 - H99	969	628	622	625
Diseases of the circulatory and respiratory	I00 - J99	1,582	1,682	1,661	1,694
Diseases of the digestive system	K00 - K93	1,076	1,154	1,154	1,180
Diseases of the genito-urinary system	N00 - N99	864	831	779	763
Complications pregnancy, birth & puerperium	O00 - P99	1,153	1,356	1,344	1,325
Diseases skin, subcutaneous tiss, musc skelet	L00 - M99	789	820	779	820
Congenital anomolies, certain perinatal conds	Q00 - Q99	305	107	99	97
Injuries and poisoning	S00 - T99	703	695	743	736
Other (not mentioned above)		820	2,060	2,442	2,366

Source: Hospital Episode Statistics   *Contact: Steve Price 020 7972 5683 (email: stephen.price@doh.gsi.gov.uk)*
See General Notes Section

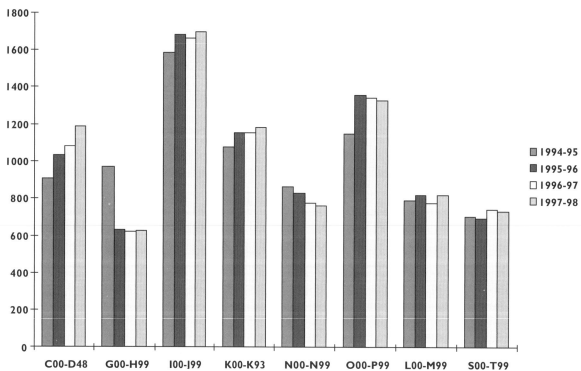

Finished consultant episodes by major diagnostic group

- ICD 10 codes replaced ICD 9 codes in 1995-96 consequently 1995-96 and 1996-97 figures are directly comparable with each offer but not with those published for earlier years.
- The total number of finished consultant episodes increased by 20% between 1994-95 and 1996-97.

Hospital Inpatient Activity: Finished consultant episodes, all specialties by age group & sex, year ending 31 March

England: NHS hospitals					Thousands
	All ages	Under 15	15-44	45-64	65 & over
1994-95					
Males	4,501	936	1,051	1,045	1,467
Females	5,959	737	2,553	1,027	1,641
Persons	10,550	1,688	3,630	2,092	3,137
1995-96					
Males	4,709	947	1,090	1,103	1,569
Females	6,199	746	2,602	1,089	1,761
Persons	11,065	1,719	3,736	2,227	3,379
1996-97					
Males	4,822	930	1,088	1,131	1,670
Females	6,375	743	2,611	1,126	1,890
Persons	11,358	1,700	3,757	2,288	3,607
1997-98					
Males	4,964	915	1,077	1,167	1,729
Females	6,580	768	2,641	1,211	2,019
Persons	11,544	1,683	3,718	2,378	3,748

Source: Hospital Episode Statistics   *Contact: Steve Price 020 7972 5683 (email: stephen.price@doh.gsi.gov.uk)*
See General Notes Section

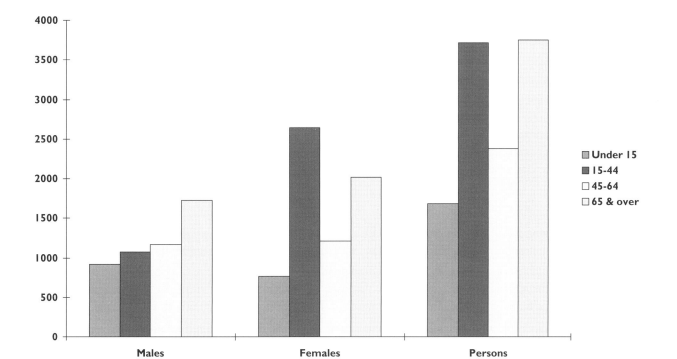

Finished consultant episodes, all specialties by age group and sex, 1997-98

- Nearly half of the finished consultant episodes for female patients in the 15-44 age group were for "Pregnancy, Childbirth and the Puerperioum".

Hospital Inpatient Activity: Finished consultant episodes, the most frequently performed operative procedures

England: NHS hospitals   **Thousands**

Both day cases & ordinary admissions combined	OPCS4R short list code(s)	1994-95	1995-96	1996-97	1997-98
Endoscopic operations upper gastrointestinal	GB2	411	453	464	453
Endoscopic operations on bladder	MC2	238	251	253	244
Extirpation of lesion of skin or tissue	HB2	159	185	212	220
Evacuation of contents of uterus	QA3	231	218	198	162
Endoscopic operations on colon	SA1	161	171	169	153
Operations for the removal of cataract	CG1,CG2	152	161	163	160
Reduction of fracture of bone	WB3	121	119	133	122
Surgical removal of tooth	FB1	97	100	92	77
Endoscopic operation on joint	WC8	89	90	86	83
Operation on inguinal hernia	TB1	86	87	79	72

Source: Hospital Episode Statistics
See General Notes Section

Contact: Steve Price 020 7972 5683 (email: stephen.price@doh.gsi.gov.uk)

Finished consultant episodes, the most frequently performed operative procedures

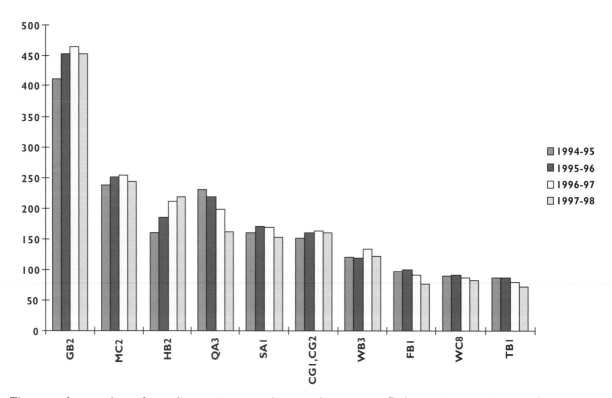

- The most frequently performed operative procedures each year were Endoscopic operations on the upper gastrointestinal tract (GB2).
- Evacuations of the contents of the uterus (QA3) was the only operative procedure that showed a year on year decrease.

Hospital Inpatient Activity: Average daily number of available beds by sector; NHS trusts

England							Thousands
Sector	1987-88	1992-93	1993-94	1994-95	1995-96	1996-97	1997-98
All specialties	**297**	**232**	**219**	**212**	**206**	**199**	**194**
Acute	128	113	110	108	108	109	108
Geriatric	53	40	37	37	34	32	30
Mental illness	67	47	44	42	39	38	37
Learning disability	33	19	16	13	13	10	8
Maternity	16	13	13	12	11	11	11

Source: KH03 return   *Contact: Mohamed Adrish 0113 2545235 (email: mohamed.adrish@doh.gsi.gov.uk)*
See General Notes Section

Average daily number of available beds; NHS trusts

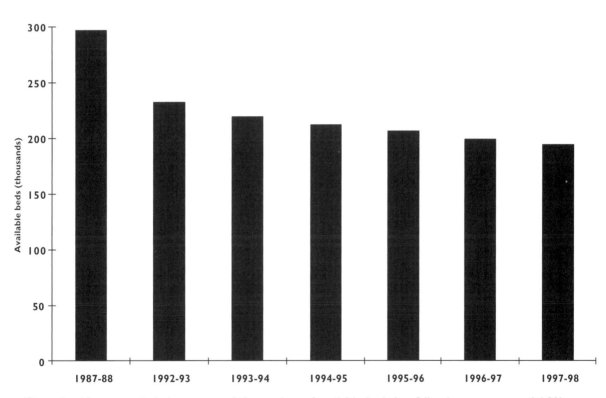

- Over the 10 year period, the average daily number of available beds has fallen by an average of 4.2% per annum.

Inpatient Waiting Lists: Patients waiting for elective admission, June 1999, variation by specialty (ordinary admissions and day cases combined)

England

Specialty	Total number waiting (thousands)	0-5	Months waiting (per cent) 6-11	12+
All specialties	**1094.3**	**74.5**	**21.0**	**4.5**
Trauma and Orthopaedics	234.0	65.5	27.1	7.3
General surgery	201.5	75.5	20.2	4.4
Ophthalmology	156.6	71.7	24.5	3.8
Ear, Nose and Throat	110.5	71.0	23.7	5.3
Obstetrics and Gynaecology	103.5	81.4	15.7	3.0
Urology	75.0	82.5	14.4	3.2
Oral surgery	44.8	79.2	18.1	2.6
Plastic surgery	38.3	70.7	24.0	5.3
Others	130.1	84.8	12.9	2.3

Percentages may not sum due to rounding.

Contact: Martin Campbell 0113 2545455
(email: martin.campbell@doh.gsi.gov.uk)

See General Notes Section

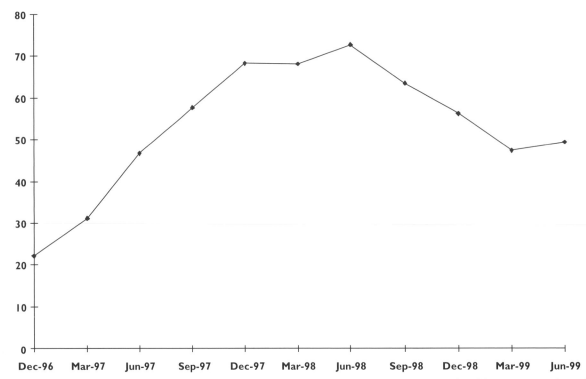

Patients waiting over 12 months

- Seven out of ten patients had been waiting less than six months, and just over half had been waiting less than three months.
- Between June 1998 and June 1999, the number of patients waiting over one year decreased by 23,300.

Hospital Outpatient Activity: Outpatient attendances by sector; NHS trusts

England							Thousands
Sector	1987-88	1992-93	1993-94	1994-95	1995-96	1996-97	1997-98
All specialties	**36,846**	**37,527**	**38,202**	**39,306**	**40,118**	**40,873**	**41,635**
Acute	31,505	32,595	33,362	34,452	35,398	36,054	36,887
Geriatric	375	452	459	480	476	492	481
Mental illness	1,611	1,812	1,883	2,009	1,998	2,104	2,126
Learning disabilities	34	44	55	58	66	67	68
Maternity	3,321	2,623	2,443	2,307	2,180	2,156	2,074

Source: KH09 return. *Contact: Mohamed Adrish 0113 2545235 (email: mohamed.adrish@doh.gsi.gov.uk)*
See General Notes Section

Outpatient attendances, NHS trusts

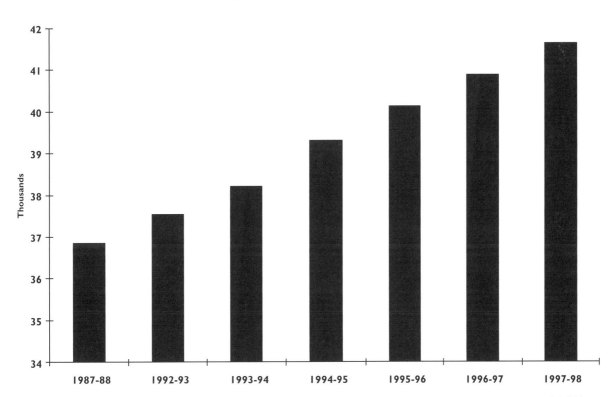

- Over the 10 year period, the total number of outpatient attendances increased by an average of 1.2% per annum.

Outpatient Waiting Times: Patients seen following GP written referral and time waited from referral to consultation - Quarter ended 30 June 1999

England

Specialty	Number seen following GP referral (thousands)		Percentage seen who waited under 13 weeks		Percentage seen who waited over 26 weeks	
	June 98	June 99	June 98	June 99	June 98	June 99
All specialties	**1,827**	**1,838**	**82**	**78**	**4**	**6**
General surgery	250	261	91	88	2	3
Urology	68	72	83	76	3	5
Trauma and Orthopaedics	174	174	66	61	11	14
Ear, Nose and Throat	163	161	76	70	4	8
Ophthalmology	158	154	72	67	6	9
Oral surgery	62	66	78	78	4	6
Plastic surgery	25	25	73	69	12	13
General medicine	121	122	88	83	2	3
Dermatology	134	133	77	73	6	7
Gynaecology	175	177	88	87	1	2

Contact: Martin Campbell 0113 2545455 (email: martin.campbell@doh.gsi.gov.uk)

See General Notes Section

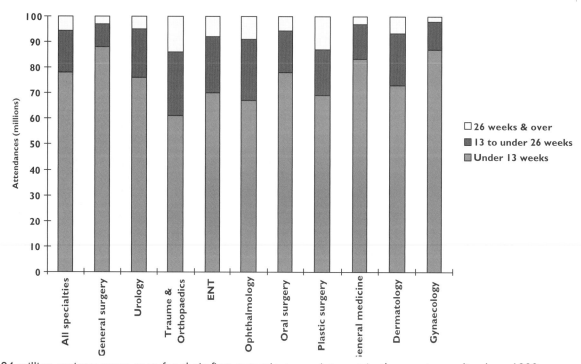

Waiting times from GP referral to first outpatient consultation for Quarter 1 1999-00

- 1.84 million patients were seen for their first outpatient appointment in the quarter ending June 1999 following referral from their GP.
- Of those seen following referral by their GP, 78% had waited less than 13 weeks and 94% had waited less than 26 weeks.
- Further information is available from Statistical Bulletin: "Waiting times for first outpatient appointments in England".

Patients Charter: Performance against key standards: Quarters ended 30 June 1998 to 30 June 1999

England					Percentages and numbers
	1998-99 Q1	1998-99 Q2	1998-99 Q3	1998-99 Q4	1999-00 Q1
Key HCHS standards					
Emergency admissions through A&E - % admitted:					
within 2 hours	82	83	79	79	82
within 2 to 4 hours	12	12	13	13	12
4 hours plus	6	5	8	8	6
Cancellation of operation - patients not admitted within 1 month of cancellation	2,174	1,495	2,472	3,239	2,384
Key FHS standards					
Medical records transfer - % within standard:					
Urgent	88	68	59	87	77
Routine	85	85	84	82	73

Percentages may not sum due to rounding. Contact: Martin Moffat 0113 2545240 (email: martin.moffat@doh.gsi.gov.uk)
See General Notes Section

Cancellation of operations - patients not admitted within 1 month of cancellation

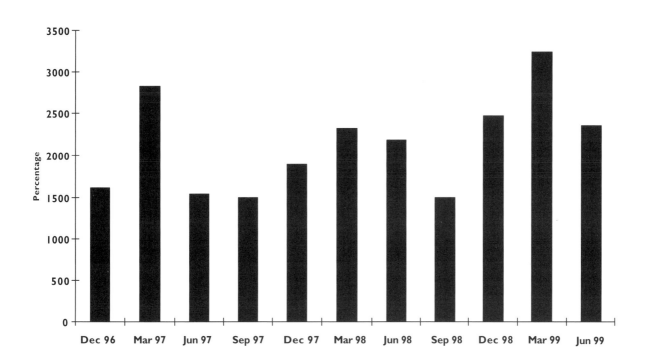

- There was a 9.7% increase in the number of patients not admitted within one month of last-minute of cancellation of an operation, from 2,174 in the first quarter of 1998-99 to 2,384 in the first quarter of 1999-00.
- Further information available from the NHS Quarterly Review.

Mental Health & Learning Disability: Hospital and community occupied bed days commissioned for people with a mental illness

England							**Millions**
Commissioned for residents of health authorities	1992-93	1993-94	1994-95	1995-96	1996-97	1997-98	1998-99
Hospital occupied bed days	14.0	12.7	12.4	12.1	11.8	11.5	11.2
Community occupied bed days	2.4	2.8	3.2	3.4	3.8	4.2	4.4

Source: Common Information Core, Outturn   *Contact: Paul Steele 0113 2546124 (email: paul.steele@doh.gsi.gov.uk)*
See General Notes Section

- Between 1992-93 and 1998-99 the number of hospital occupied bed days commissioned for people with a mental illness fell by 20% to 11.2 million.
- During the same period, occupied bed days commissioned in the community for people with a mental illness rose by 85% to 4.4 million.

Mental Health & Learning Disability: Hospital beds & places in residential & nursing care homes for people with learning disabilities

England						Numbers
	1992-93	1993-94	1994-95	1995-96	1996-97	1997-98
Average daily available NHS beds	**18,520**	**16,270**	**13,210**	**12,680**	**13,040**	**12,280**
For children	410	410	410	370	400	380
For other ages						
secure units	300	290	330	330	420	440
short stay	1,250	1,320	1,410	1,630	1,350	1,440
long stay	16,560	14,250	11,060	10,350	7,440	5,940
Residential facilities	.	.	.	.	3,430	4,080
Beds in private nursing homes, hospitals etc.	**2,850**	**3,100**	**3,200**	**3320**	**3,360**	**3,580**
Children	50	110	100	70	60	70
Other ages	2,800	2,990	3,100	3,250	3,300	3,510
Staffed residential home places for adults	**34,450**	**35,010**	**36,290**	**38,170**	**40,500**	**41,610**
Local authority	10,890	10,120	9,670	9,340	8,190	8,200
Voluntary	12,510	13,000	13,940	14,650	15,070	16,740
Private	11,040	11,890	12,680	14,190	17,230	16,660
Staffed residential home places for children	**2,110**	**2,000**	**1,760**	**1,770**	**1,480**	**1,810**

Source: KH03, KO36, RA (previously RAC5 & RAC5(S))

Contact: Paul Thatti 020 7972 5546 (email: paul.thatti@doh.gsi.gov.uk)

See General Notes Section

Hospital beds/places in residential & nursing homes for people with learning disabilties,1997-98

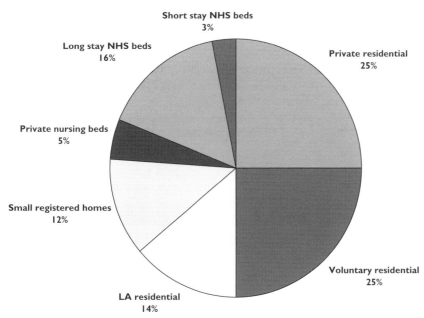

- NHS residential facilities were recorded separately for the first time in 1996-97. Some of these beds may have been recorded under other headings.
- The long term downward trend in the average number of beds available in NHS facilities has leveled out in the last four years.
- The number of places in staffed residential homes has increased by about 7,000 in the five years to 1997-98.

Mental Health & Learning Disability: Hospital beds & places in residential & nursing care homes for people with mental illness

England   Numbers

	1992-93	1993-94	1994-95	1995-96	1996-97	1997-98
Average daily available NHS beds	**47,310**	**43,530**	**41,830**	**39,480**	**38,780**	**37,880**
For children	640	600	550	570	540	520
For elderly						
short stay	5,770	6,240	6,390	6,390	7,370	7,380
long stay	13,660	12,110	10,760	9,330	8,230	7,410
For other ages						
secure units	930	1,030	1,080	1,370	1,580	1,920
short stay	15,300	14,680	15,210	15,080	14,500	14,460
long stay	11,000	8,870	7,830	6,730	5,410	4,910
Residential facilities	.	.	.	.	1,160	1,280
Beds in private nursing homes, hospitals etc.	**16,950**	**21,080**	**24,190**	**27,450**	**28,510**	**28,280**
Elderly	12,400	16,330	19,330	22,140	21,450	19,130
Other ages (including children)	4,550	4,750	4,860	5,300	7,050	9,150
Staffed residential home places for adults	**21,130**	**21,650**	**22,180**	**24,030**	**34,250**	**35,370**
Elderly	8,830	8,910	9,220	10,670	19,260	21,040
Other ages	12,300	12,740	12,960	13,370	14,990	14,940
Small registered residential home places	.	**1,130**	**1,610**	**1,910**	**2,690**	**2,580**

Source: KH03, KO36, RA (previously RAC5 & RAC5(S))   *Contact: Paul Thatti 020 7972 5546 (email: paul.thatti@doh.gsi.gov.uk)*

See General Notes Section

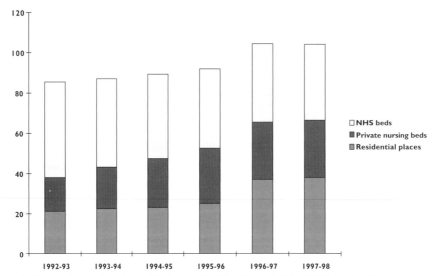

Hospital beds & places in residential & nursing homes for people with mental illness

- The average daily number of beds available in NHS facilities fell by 20% in the five years to 1997-98 - a fall of 9,400 beds.
- Long stay NHS beds for elderly patients fell by almost 6,250; long stay beds for other adults fell by 6,100. Some of these may now be recorded as residential beds - 1,280 in 1997-98.
- The number of beds available in private nursing homes, hospital and clinics increased by almost 70% between 1992-93 and 1997-98 - an increase of 14,850 places most of which was for elderly patients.
- The increase in the number of residential places for elderly mentally ill people between 1995-96 and 1996-97 (10,220) was a result of a reclassification of some homes rather than a real increase.

Mental Health & Learning Disability: Admissions to NHS hospitals under a learning disability specialty by sex and age group

England						Rate per 1,000 population	
	1991-92	1992-93	1993-94	1994-95	1995-96	1996-97 Prov.	1997-98 Prov.
Males all ages	**1.1**	**1.2**	**1.2**	**1.2**	**1.2**	**1.2**	**1.1**
Under 15	1.2	1.6	1.7	1.9	2.1	2.1	1.8
15-19	2.6	3.0	3.0	2.7	2.7	3.0	2.7
20-24	2.9	2.6	2.6	2.7	2.3	2.5	2.1
25-44	1.4	1.3	1.3	1.3	1.2	1.2	1.2
45-64	0.3	0.3	0.3	0.3	0.3	0.3	0.3
65 & over	0.1	0.0	0.1	0.0	0.1	0.1	0.1
Females all ages	**0.9**	**0.9**	**1.0**	**1.0**	**0.9**	**1.0**	**1.0**
Under 15	0.9	1.1	1.2	1.5	1.5	1.6	1.6
15-19	1.7	2.0	2.2	2.1	2.1	2.2	2.6
20-24	2.6	2.6	2.6	2.4	1.9	1.9	2.1
25-44	1.1	1.2	1.2	1.2	1.1	1.2	1.2
45-64	0.4	0.4	0.4	0.3	0.3	0.3	0.3
65 & over	0.1	0.1	0.1	0.1	0.1	0.1	0.0

Source: Hospital Episode Statistics   *Contact: Paul Thatti 020 7972 5546 (email: paul.thatti@doh.gsi.gov.uk)*

Admissions to NHS hospitals under mental handicap specialty by sex and age group 1997-98

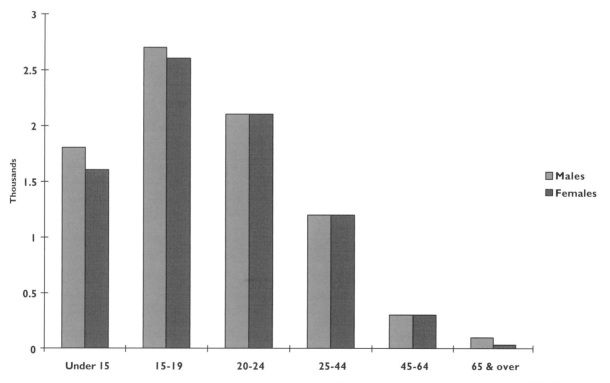

- Rates of admission to the mental handicap specialty were higher for men than for women in 1997-98.
- Admission rates were highest in the 15-19 age group.

Mental Health & Learning Disability: Admissions to NHS hospitals under mental illness specialty by sex and age group

England						Rate per 1,000 population	
	1991-92	1992-93	1993-94	1994-95	1995-96	1996-97 Prov.	1997-98 Prov.
All ages	**4.2**	**4.3**	**4.5**	**4.4**	**4.4**	**4.4**	**4.3**
Under 15	0.2	0.2	0.3	0.3	0.1	0.2	0.1
15-19	1.7	1.8	2.0	1.9	2.0	2.1	2.1
20-24	3.7	4.0	4.2	4.4	4.6	4.8	5.0
25-44	4.7	5.0	5.3	5.2	5.3	5.4	5.5
45-64	4.0	4.0	4.0	3.9	3.7	3.7	3.7
65-74	5.9	6.0	6.0	6.2	5.8	5.7	5.3
75-84	12.2	13.0	13.1	13.4	12.8	12.3	11.3
85 & over	16.4	17.9	18.1	18.4	18.2	17.0	15.6

Source: Hospital Episode Statistics   *Contact: Paul Thatti 020 7972 5545 (email: paul.thatti@doh.gsi.gov.uk)*

Admissions to NHS hospitals under mental illness specialties by sex and age group, 1997-98

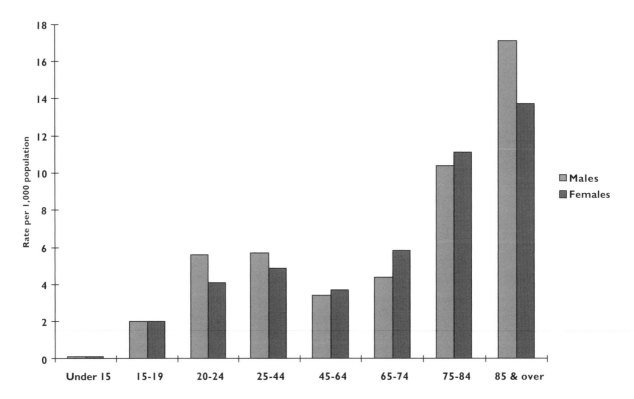

- Rates of admission to mental illness specialty care are highest in the older age groups.
- The highest rates are for men aged 85 & over (20.1 per 1,000 population in 1996-97).
- In younger age groups, rates of admission tend to be higher for men than women.

Mental Health & Learning Disability: Other NHS activity

England							Thousands
	1987-88	1992-93	1993-94	1994-95	1995-96	1996-97	1997-98
Consultant outpatient first attendance							
Mental handicap(learning disability)	4	4	5	5	5	6	6
Mental illness	207	238	245	257	271	285	290
Ward attenders							
Learning disabilities	28	14	11	17	16	15	11
Mental illness	149	124	109	116	104	102	93
First patient contacts with clinical							
psychology & community nursing services							
Community mental handicap nursing	..	40	44	45	47	52	55
Clinical psychology services	..	191	202	221	227	244	257
Community psychiatric nursing	..	406	475	493	530	567	584
First attendances at NHS day care facilities							
Learning disabilities	..	4	5	6	7	9	6
Mental illness	..	60	66	63	66	65	62
Old age psychiatry	..	28	35	31	32	34	32
Child and adolescent psychiatry	..	3	4	3	2	2	2

Source: KH09, KH05, KC58, KC57, KT24, KH14   *Contact: Paul Thatti 020 7972 5546 (email: paul.thatti@doh.gsi.gov.uk)*

- First outpatient attendances to mental illness specialties have increased by 20% in the last five years.
- First contacts in each year with community psychiatric nurses increased by 40% between in the last five years.
- First contacts in each year with clinical psychology services increased by 30% in the last five years.
- First contacts in each year with community mental handicap nurses increased by 40% in the last five years.

Children

1. Looked after by local authorities
2. Children and young people on child protection registers
3. Adoptions from care
4. Aged 16 and over who ceased to be looked after by a local authority

Adults

5. Contact hours of home help and home care provided
6. Home help and home care trends
7. Local authority supported residents in residential and nursing care

TABLE CI

Children: Looked after by local authorities at 31 March

England   **Numbers**

	1995	1996	1997	1998	1999
Total	**49,800**	**50,600**	**51,400**	**53,300**	**55,300**
Rate per 10,000 population under 18	**45**	**45**	**46**	**47**	**49**
Age groups					
Under 1	1,600	1,600	1,700	1,800	2,100
1-4	6,800	7,400	8,200	8,800	9,300
5-9	10,100	10,500	10,900	11,700	12,500
10-15	21,800	21,700	21,400	21,700	22,300
16 & over	9,500	9,400	9,100	9,400	9,000
Placement					
Foster placements	32,100	33,000	33,500	35,100	36,100
Community homes	5,900	5,400	5,200	4,900	4,800
Schools and associated homes and hostels	920	950	970	970	1,000
Placed with own parents	4,400	4,700	5,200	5,600	6,200
Placed for adoption	2,200	2,200	2,400	2,500	2,900
Other placements	4,300	4,400	4,100	4,200	4,300

Figures include estimates for some local authorities.　　　　*Contact: Steve Maslen 020 7972 5799*
Figures may not add due to rounding.　　　　　　　　　*(email: steve.maslen@doh.gsi.gov.uk)*

See General Notes Section

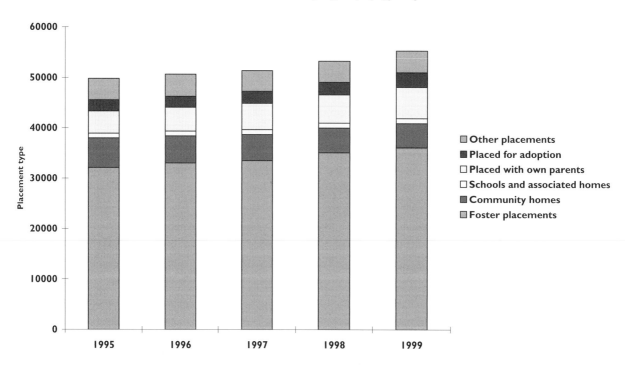

Children looked after at 31 March, England, by type of placement

- 55,300 children were looked after in England at 31 March 1999, 4% more than a year earlier, and representing 49 per 10,000 children under 18.
- 55% were boys, compared with 51% of all children aged under 18 years.
- 36,100 children were looked after in foster placements - 3% more than a year earlier.

Children: Children and young people on child protection registers at 31 March

England   **Numbers**

	1995	1996	1997	1998	1999
Total	**35,000**	**32,400**	**32,400**	**31,600**	**31,900**
Sex					
Boys	17,600	16,200	16,400	16,000	16,000
Girls	17,200	16,000	15,700	15,500	15,600
Category of abuse					
Neglect	11,200	11,200	12,200	13,000	13,900
Physical	13,000	11,400	10,900	9,900	9,100
Sexual	9,200	7,700	7,400	6,700	6,600
Emotional	4,700	5,000	5,000	5,200	5,400
Other	300	700	600	500	700

Includes estimates for some local authorities.
Figures may not add due to rounding.

Contact: Mike Cornish 020 7972 5573
(email: mike.cornish@doh.gsi.gov.uk)

See General Notes Section

Percentage of children on child protection registers at 31 March 1999 by category of abuse

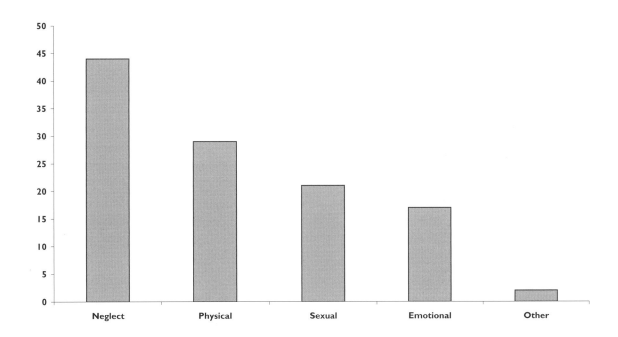

- At 31 March 1999 there were 31,900 children on child protection registers in England.
- This figure represents 28 children in every 10,000.
- Slightly more boys were on the register than girls in 1999; girls out-numbered boys before 1994.
- The numbers at risk from physical or sexual abuse continue to fall while the numbers at risk from neglect and emotional abuse are rising steadily.

TABLE C3

Children: Adoptions from care

England **Numbers**

	1994	1995	1996	1997	1998
Total	**2,300**	**2,100**	**1,900**	**1,900**	**2,000**
Sex					
Boys	1,200	1,000	990	930	1,000
Girls	1,100	1,000	940	950	980
Age at adoption					
Under 1	210	210	150	140	150
1-4	910	830	870	890	1,000
5-9	790	700	620	590	630
10-15	340	290	260	220	160
16 & over	50	30	30	30	30
Duration of final period of care					
Under 1 year	250	230	190	180	170
1 year to under 2 years	400	370	410	390	420
2 years to under 3 years	540	390	410	490	570
3 years & over	1,100	1,100	920	820	850

Figures may not add, due to rounding.

See General Notes Section

Contact: Steve Maslen 020 7972 5799
(email: steve.maslen@doh.gsi.gov.uk)

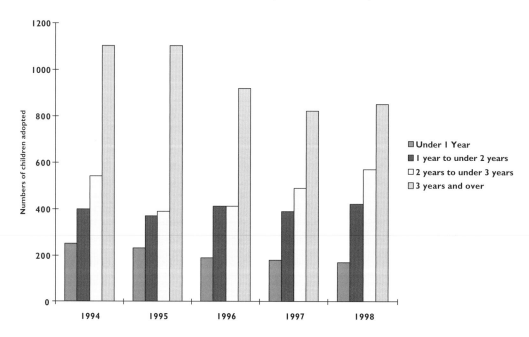

Looked-after children who were adopted, England: duration of final period of care

- Roughly a third of all children adopted in England had been looked after by a local authority immediately prior to being adopted. The remaining two thirds are adopted by step-parents or relatives, and are not included in this table.
- The average age of looked-after children who are adopted fell from 5 years 11 months in 1993/4, to 4 years 11 months in 1997/98.
- The proportion of looked-after children who were freed for adoption before being adopted has risen from 21% in 1993/94, to 32% in 1997/98.

Children: Aged 16 and over who ceased to be looked after by a local authority

England					Numbers
	1994	1995	1996	1997	1998
All children	**9,000**	**8,800**	**8,700**	**8,300**	**7,800**
Age on ceasing					
16	3,000	3,400	3,500	3,400	3,600
17	1,500	1,400	1,500	1,500	1,400
18th birthday	4,300	3,900	3,500	3,300	2,700
Older than 18th birthday	180	160	100	100	130
Final placement					
Foster placement	3,300	3,600	3,600	3,700	3,600
Childrens homes	2,300	2,200	2,100	1,900	1,800
Living independently	2,100	1,900	1,700	1,600	1,300
Placed with own parents	570	490	480	450	500
Other placement	740	740	740	670	570

Figures may not add up due to rounding

See General Notes Section

Contact: Steve Maslen 020 7972 5689
(email: steve.maslen@doh.gsi.gov.uk)

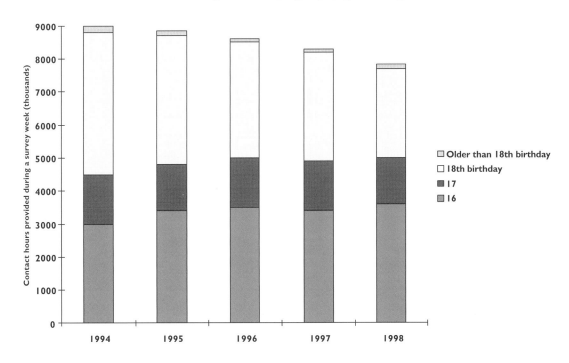

Care leavers aged 16 or over, England, by age on ceasing

Legend:
- Older than 18th birthday
- 18th birthday
- 17
- 16

- 47% of young people leaving care aged 16 or over had been living in foster placements, and a further 23% in childrens homes and hostels.
- Half of care leavers aged 16 or over had been looked after continuously for more than two years, although a quarter had been looked after more less than six months.
- The number of care leavers aged 16 or over has been falling since 1993/94.

Adults: Contact hours of home help and home care provided, by sector

England: Survey week in September/October — Numbers

	1994	1995	1996	1997	1998(p)
Contact hours - provided by					
Local authority	1,787,000	1,688,900	1,581,200	1,506,500	1,391,800
Independent	428,200	706,800	900,900	1,130,800	1,180,400
Households receiving home help/home care					
Local authority	479,300	419,600	370,200	335,100	283,100
Independent	59,600	93,900	121,000	144,000	162,800

Figures are rounded to the nearest 100.
(p) = provisional
See General Notes Section

Contact: Thereza Irvine-Hendrix 020 7972 5591
(email: thereza.irvine-hendrix@doh.gsi.gov.uk)

Number of contact hours for home help and home care (thousands)

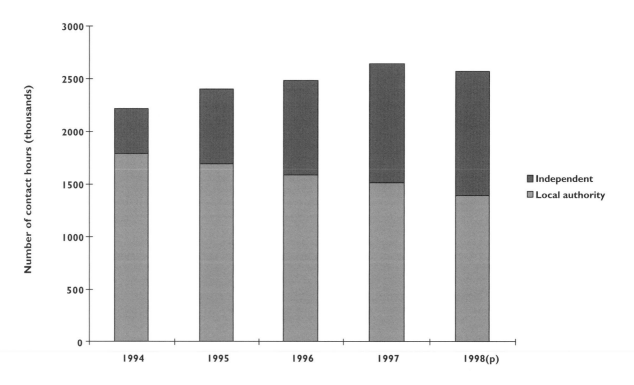

- In 1998(p) over 2.5 million contact hours of home help and home care were provided to around 446,000 households.
- The number of contact hours provided by the independent sector continues to increase, but at a slower rate between 1997 and 1998 than that observed in previous years.
- The number of contact hours provided directly by local authorities has fallen by 22% since 1994.

Adults: Home help and home care trends (all sectors)

England: Survey week in September/October					Index 1994=100
	1994	1995	1996	1997	1998(p)
Contact hours	100	108	112	119	116
Households receiving services	100	95	91	89	83
Average contact hours per household	100	114	123	134	140

(p) = provisional

Contact:Thereza Irvine Hendrix 020 7972 5591
(email: thereza.irvine-hendrix@doh.gsi.gov.uk)

See General Notes Section

Trends in home help and home care

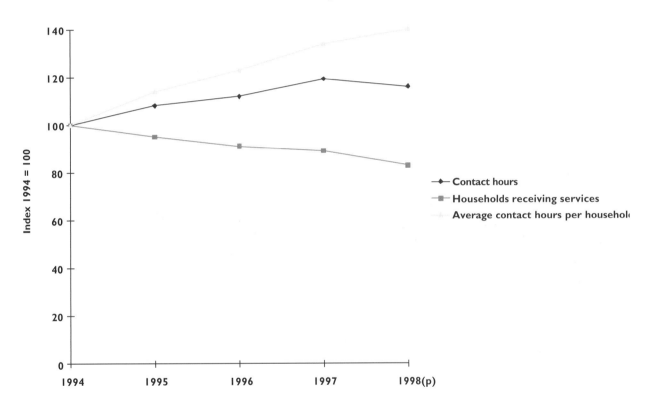

- Home help carers are spending more time with each of their clients - the average number of contact hours has increased by 40% since 1994.
- Although the number of households receiving services has decreased over the period 1994-1998, the number of contact hours increased until 1997.

Adults: Local authority supported residents in staffed residential and nursing care at 31 March

England   Numbers

	1994	1995	1996	1997	1998
All staffed homes	**144,312**	**180,718**	**210,410**	**236,335**	**249,438**
Local authority staffed	70,444	67,327	61,943	58,747	54,611
Independent residential care	48,714	70,153	91,221	111,530	121,923
Independent nursing care	25,154	43,238	57,246	66,058	72,904
People aged 65 and over	112,939	142,994	168,962	190,145	202,722
People aged under 65					
Physically/sensorily disabled adults	7,757	9,338	9,344	10,356	8,734
People with mental health problems	4,432	5,815	7,370	7,965	9,277
People with learning disabilities	17,648	20,590	22,811	25,446	26,029
Other people	1,536	1,981	1,923	2,423	2,676

Contact: Thereza Irvine-Hendrix 020 7972 5591
(email: thereza.irvine-hendrix@doh.gsi.gov.uk)

See General Notes Section

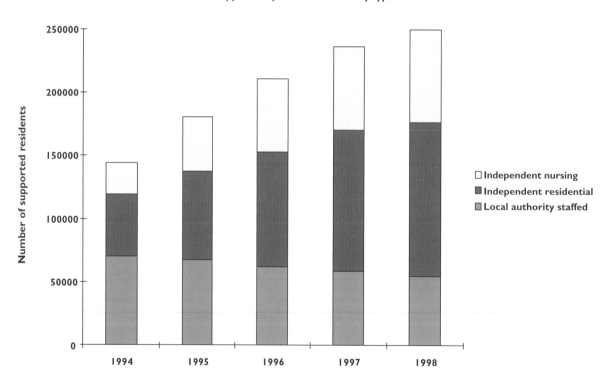

Residents supported by local authorities by type of home

- The number of supported residents in staffed residential and nursing care increased from 236,300 to 249,400 between 1997 and 1998. This increase of about 6% is considerably less than the year on year observed increases in previous years.
- 49% were in independent residential care homes and 29% were in independent nursing homes and 22% per cent were in local authority staffed homes.
- Between 1997 and 1998 an increase in supported residents was observed for all client groups, except for physically/sensory disabled adults.

NHS Hospital and Community Health Services

1. Directly employed staff by main staff groups
2. Medical and dental staff
3. Directly employed staff by sex
4. Directly employed staff by ethnic group

NHS General Medical Services

5. General medical practitioners (GPs) and practice staff employed by GPs
6. Unrestricted Principals and Equivalents by contractual commitment

Other

7. General Dental and Ophthalmic Services
8. Staff of local authority social services departments

NHS Hospital and Community Health Services: Directly employed staff by main staff groups at 30 September

England						Whole-time equivalent (thousands)	
	1988	1993	1994	1995	1996	1997	1998
All directly employed staff	**787.2**	**769.1**	**758.5**	**755.6**	**761.3**	**758.1**	**765.9**
All direct care staff	..	..	..	497.3	507.9	508.3	517.3
Nursing, midwifery and health visiting staff	..	..	..	330.4	332.7	330.6	332.2
of which: qualified staff	..	..	..	246.8	248.1	246.0	247.2
Medical and dental staff	42.8	48.7	49.4	52.6	54.2	57.1	58.7
Other direct care staff	..	..	..	111.6	118.5	120.6	126.4
All management and support staff	..	..	..	260.9	255.9	249.7	248.6
Administration and estates staff	..	..	..	168.7	167.4	167.0	167.7
Other management & support staff	..	..	..	92.2	88.4	82.8	80.9

Contact: Lucy Jack 0113 2545902 (email: lucy.jack@doh.gsi.gov.uk)

See General Notes Section

NHS HCHS directly employed staff by main staff groups, 1998

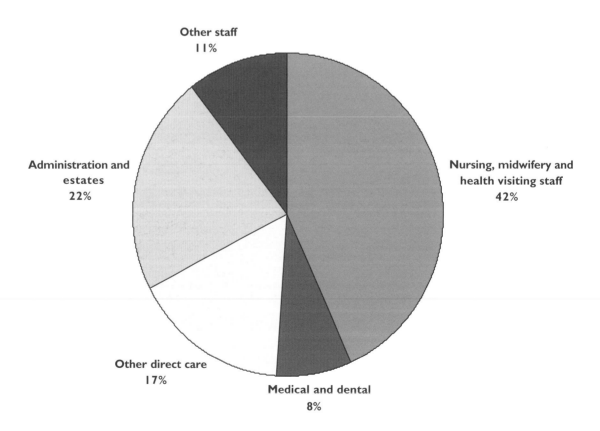

- Nearly one million people are directly employed by the NHS hospital and community health services - equivalent to 766,000 whole-time equivalents.
- 68% of these staff were direct care staff and 32% were management and support staff.

NHS Hospital and Community Health Services: Medical and dental staff at 30 September 1998

England						Whole-time equivalent (thousands)	
	1988	1993	1994	1995	1996	1997	1998
All medical and dental staff	**42.8**	**48.7**	**49.3**	**52.6**	**54.2**	**57.1**	**58.7**
Hospital medical staff	**37.6**	**43.8**	**44.7**	**47.9**	**49.7**	**52.7**	**54.4**
Consultants	13.2	15.2	15.6	16.9	17.6	18.6	19.4
Other career grades	0.7	1.9	2.0	2.6	3.0	3.4	4.1
Registrar group	8.8	9.8	10.0	10.3	10.2	10.8	11.1
Other junior grades	12.7	15.0	15.1	16.1	16.9	17.8	18.0
Other hospital grades	2.2	2.0	1.8	2.1	2.0	2.0	1.8
Other medical and dental staff	**5.2**	**4.9**	**4.7**	**4.7**	**4.6**	**4.4**	**4.3**

Contact: David Hubbard 0113 2545888 (email: david.hubbard@doh.gsi.gov.uk)

NHS HCHS hospital consultants and junior doctors, 1998

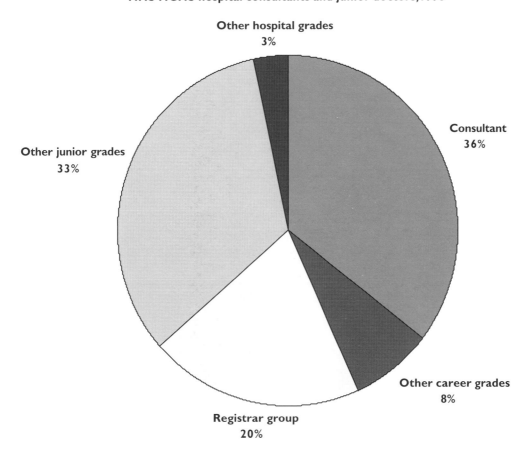

- In the 10 year period from 1988, the number of hospital medical consultants has grown at an average annual rate of 3.9% per annum, while the number of junior doctors has grown at an average annual rate of 3.1%.

NHS Hospital and Community Health Services: Directly employed staff by sex at 30 September 1998

England		Percentages
	Males	Females
All directly employed staff	**24.5**	**75.5**
Nursing, midwifery and health visiting staff	12.2	87.8
of which : qualified	11.4	88.6
Medical and dental staff	66.6	33.4
Other direct care staff	23.7	76.3
Administration and estates staff	25.1	74.9
Other management & support staff	42.5	57.5

Contact: Lucy Jack 0113 2545902 (email: lucy.jack@doh.gsi.gov.uk)

See General Notes Section

NHS HCHS Directly employed staff by sex, 1998

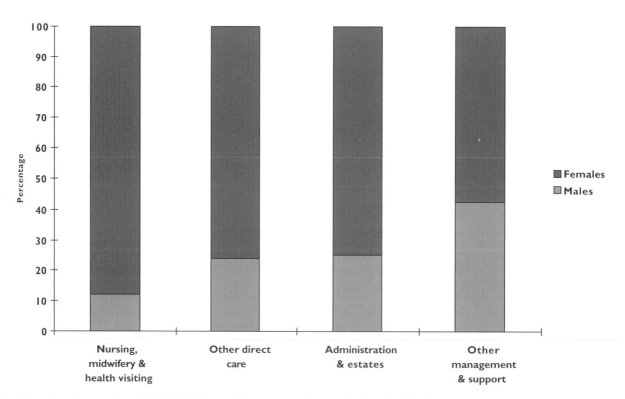

- The directly employed NHS HCHS workforce is predominantly female (76%) although the proportion is smaller for some staff groups e.g. 33% for medical and dental staff.

NHS Hospital and Community Health Services: Directly employed staff by ethnic group at 30 September 1998

England					Percentages
	White	Black	Asian	Other	Unknown
All directly employed staff	**87.1**	**3.1**	**3.2**	**2.6**	**4.0**
Nursing, midwifery and health visiting staff	86.4	3.9	1.3	2.4	6.0
of which : qualified staff	87.4	4.0	1.5	2.5	4.6
Medical and dental staff	64.7	3.9	17.3	8.3	5.8
Other direct care staff	89.9	4.6	1.7	1.8	1.9
Administration and estates staff	93.4	2.0	1.6	1.3	1.7
Other management & support staff	92.2	2.8	1.0	2.0	2.0

Contact: Lucy Jack   0113 2545902 (email: lucy.jack@doh.gsi.gov.uk)

See General Notes Section

NHS HCHS directly employed staff by ethnic origin, 1998

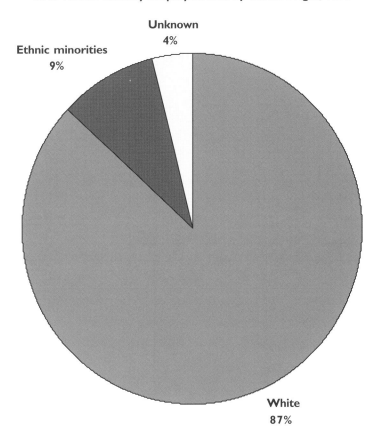

Unknown
4%

Ethnic minorities
9%

White
87%

- Over 6% of NHS directly employed non-medical staff are from ethnic minority groups - broadly in line with the working population of England.

NHS General Medical Services: General medical practitioners (GPs) and practice staff employed by GPs at 1 October

England	Practitioners and practice staff (numbers and whole time equivalents, thousands)						
	1988	1993	1994	1995	1996	1997	1998
Total practitioners	**27.4**	**28.5**	**28.7**	**28.9**	**29.1**	**29.4**	**29.7**
of which UPEs	25.3	26.3	26.6	26.7	26.9	27.1	27.4
of which GMS UPs	25.3	26.3	26.6	26.7	26.9	27.1	27.0
Restricted principals	0.2	0.1	0.1	0.1	0.1	0.1	0.1
Assistants	0.3	0.5	0.6	0.6	0.8	0.8	0.7
GP registrars	1.7	1.5	1.4	1.4	1.3	1.3	1.4
of which GMS GP Registrars	1.7	1.5	1.4	1.4	1.3	1.3	1.4
Salaried doctors (Para 52 SFA)	..	..	..	..	..	..	0.1
Estimated WTE UPEs	..	25.4	25.5	25.6	25.6	25.7	25.8
All Practice Staff	57.2	84.2	84.2	97.8	97.4	100.0	101.0
of which GMS Practice Staff	57.2	84.2	84.2	97.8	97.4	100.0	99.5
All WTE Practice Staff	33.7	54.0	51.8	59.3	59.3	60.6	61.3
Practice nurse	3.5	9.6	9.1	9.7	9.8	10.1	10.4
Direct Patient Care	0.4	1.2	1.2	1.6	1.5	1.5	1.7
Admin & Clerical	24.6	42.3	41.3	47.4	47.6	48.3	48.9
Others	5.2	0.8	0.2	0.6	0.4	0.6	0.3

Contact: Malcolm Dudlyke 0113 2545804 (email malcolm.dudlyke@doh.gsi.gov.uk)

- UPEs (Unrestricted Principals and Equivalents) includes Unrestricted Principles (UPs), PMS contracted GPs and PMS salaried GPs.
- Total Practitioners also includes "Other PMS" doctors (not shown separately above) who work in PMS pilots and are the equivalents of Assistants or Salaried Doctors. In 1998 there were 9.
- Estimated whole-time equivalent (WTE) UPEs are calculated based on the results of the 1992-93 GMP Workload Survey using factors of: 1.00 full time UPEs; 0.69 three quarter time; 0.65 job share; 0.60 half time.
- WTE practice staff total for 1998 does not include 62 WTE community nurses who are seconded to PMS Pilots. These are however included in the total practice staff number.

TABLE D6

NHS General Medical Services: UPEs by contractual commitment at 1 October

England						Thousands and percentages
	1993	1994	1995	1996	1997	1998
All UPEs (thousands)	**26.3**	**26.6**	**26.7**	**26.9**	**27.1**	**27.4**
of which:						
Full time	23.7	23.6	23.4	23.2	23.0	23.0
Job share	0.5	0.6	0.6	0.6	0.6	0.5
1/2 time	0.8	1.0	1.1	1.4	1.6	1.8
3/4 time	1.3	1.4	1.5	1.7	1.9	2.1

Contact: Malcolm Dudlyke 0113 2545804 (email: malcolm.dudlyke@doh.gsi.gov.uk)

UPEs by contractual commitment

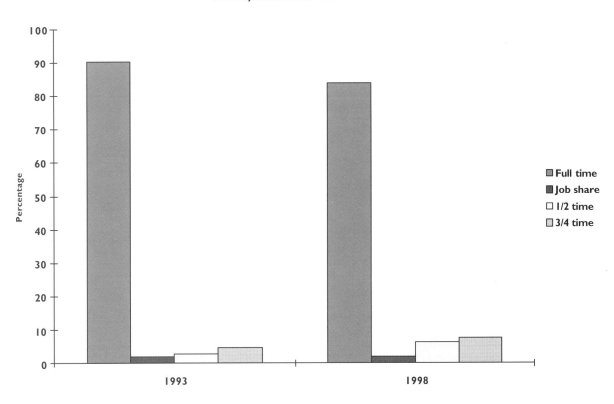

• UPEs (Unrestricted Principals and Equivalents) include Unrestricted Principals (UPs), PMS Contracted GPs and PMS Salaried GPs.

TABLE D7

General Dental and Ophthalmic Services

England						Number
	1993-94	1994-95	1995-96	1996-97	1997-98	1998-99
Number of dentists (1)						
Total	15,773	15,885	15,951	16,336	16,728	17,245
of which principals (2)	15,143	15,084	15,064	15,280	15,509	15,820
Number of ophthalmic practitioners (3)						
Ophthalmic medical practitioners	705	650	658	675	696	733
Optometrists	5,914	5,972	6,120	6,264	6,395	6,572

Contact: GDS – Sharon Lea 020 7972 5392
(email: sharon.lea@doh.gsi.gov.uk) / GOS –
Helen Dixon 020 7972 5507
(email: helen.dixon@doh.gsi.gov.uk)

See General Notes Section

Staff of local authority social services departments at 30 September

England				Whole-time equivalent (thousands)	
	1994	1995	1996	1997	1998
Total	**238**	**234**	**234**	**229**	**224**
Area office/field work staff	117	117	116	115	112
Residential care staff	72	69	68	65	62
Day care staff	31	31	32	31	30
Central/strategic HQ staff	15	15	16	16	17
Other staff not included elsewhere	3	2	2	2	2

Source: SSDS001 return   *Contact: Brian Allen 020 7972 5595 (email: brian.allen@doh.gsi.gov.uk)*

Staff of local authority social services departments at 30 September 1998

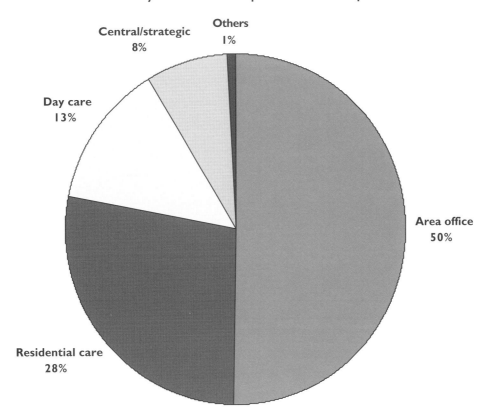

- In September 1998, local authority social services departments in England employed staff with a whole-time equivalent of 223,500.
- This represents a drop of about 3% in numbers employed by local authorities since September 1997 and 6% since September 1994.
- Nearly half of all staff work in an area office or field work setting.
- Just over a quarter of staff work in residential care.

SECTION E   EXPENDITURE

1. Actual expenditure on the NHS
2. Trend in actual gross expenditure on the NHS
3. Analysis of health authority and NHS trust expenditure
4. Historical trend in local authority personal social services gross expenditure
5. Local authority personal social services gross expenditure by client group

Actual expenditure on the NHS, 1997-98

England £ millions

	HCHS, FHS (cash Ltd) and related services	Family health services (non cash limited)	Department administration	Central health/ misc. services	NHS total
Current					
Net spending	24,872	7,930	268	505	33,575
Charges & receipts	1,780	734	27	114	2,656
Total spending	26,651	8,664	295	619	36,230
Capital					
Net spending	1,068	-	13	8	1,089
Charges & receipts	471	-	0	0	471
Total spending	1,539	-	13	8	1,560
Total					
Net spending	25,940	7,930	281	513	34,664
Charges & receipts	2,250	734	28	114	3,127
Total spending	28,190	8,664	309	627	37,791

Source: Department of Health   *Contact: Karl Payne 0113 2545368 (email: karl.payne@doh.gsi.gov.uk)*

- Nearly three quarters of NHS expenditure is spent on hospitals and community health services.
- Nearly a quarter of NHS expenditure is spent on family health services.

Trend of actual gross expenditure on the NHS, 1994-95 to 1997-98

England				£ millions
	1994-95	1995-96	1996-97	1997-98
NHS total	**32,890**	**34,430**	**35,729**	**37,791**
Hospital & community health services* (current)	22,624	23,804	24,882	26,651
Family health services (non cash limited, current)	7,327	7,698	8,190	8,664
Central health/miscellaneous services (current)	530	579	616	619
Departmental administration (current)	336	332	306	295
Capital	2,073	2,018	1,734	1,560

*Source: Department of Health, * includes cash limited FHS*

Contact: Karl Payne 0113 2545368
(email: karl.payne@doh.gsi.gov.uk)

Actual gross expenditure on the NHS, 1997-98

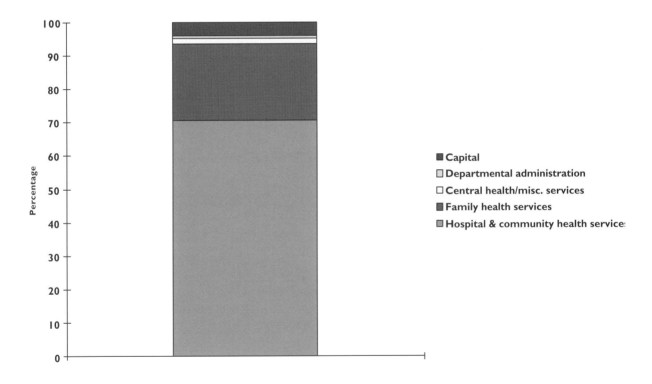

■ Capital
□ Departmental administration
□ Central health/misc. services
■ Family health services
▨ Hospital & community health service

Analysis of health authority and NHS trust expenditure (year end 31 March)

England   **£ millions**

	1994	1995	1996	1997	1998
Revenue expenditure	**22,096**	**22,573**	**23,890**	**24,128**	**25,329**
of which:					
Salaries and wages	13,913	14,303	14,961	15,580	16,099
Supplies and services - clinical	2,053	2,219	2,410	2,599	2,849
Supplies and services - general	464	482	507	523	634
Establishment	637	670	703	700	869
Transport and moveable plant	115	121	132	141	n/a
Premises and fixed plant	1,455	1,576	1,600	1,592	1,560
Miscellaneous expenditure	1,470	1,391	1,510	1,069	1,145
Capital	1,558	1,107	1,157	1,069	1,065
Purchase of health care from non-NHS bodies	325	586	731	726	1,108
External contract staff	106	118	178	129	n/a

Contact: Susan Betts 0113 2545399 (email: susan.betts@doh.gsi.gov.uk)

See General Notes Section

Analysis of health authority and NHS trust expenditure year end 31 March 1998

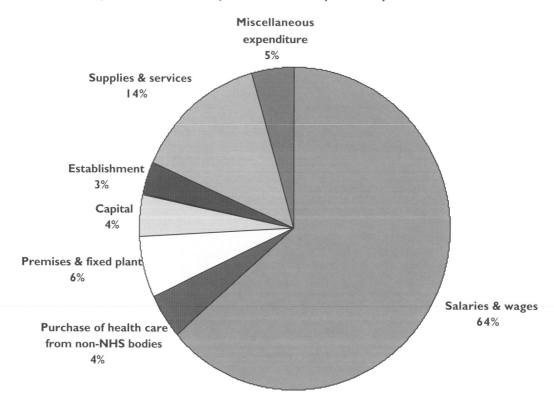

- Around 35 major capital schemes reached practical completion during 1997-98.
- During 1998-99 NHS Supplies negotiated, on behalf of the NHS, purchasing savings of £105 million.
- The weighted average pay settlement for all staff in the NHS for the year 1997-98 was 3.8%.

TABLE E4

Historical trend in local authority personal social services gross expenditure

England

£ billions

Year	Cash terms	1997-98 Prices (GDP)
1987-88	3.4	5.2
1988-89	3.8	5.4
1989-90	4.2	5.6
1990-91	4.7	5.8
1991-92	5.1	6.0
1992-93	5.5	6.2
1993-94	6.3	6.9
1994-95	7.5	8.2
1995-96	8.4	8.9
1996-97	9.3	9.5
1997-98	10.0	10.0

Contact: Brian Allen 020 7972 5595 (email: brian.allen@doh.gsi.gov.uk)

See General Notes Section

Growth in local authority personal social services gross expenditure (1987-88=100)

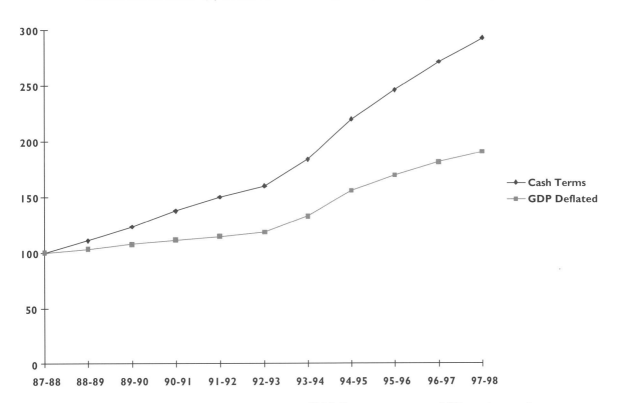

- In 1997-98, gross expenditure in England was almost £10 billion, an increase of 8% on the previous year.
- Over the ten year period from 1987-88, gross expenditure has almost trebled in cash terms and increased 90% in real terms .
- The rise in expenditure since 1993-94 includes the effects of local authorities meeting their new community care responsibilities.

Local authority personal social services gross expenditure by client group, 1997-98

England £ millions

	Elderly	Children	Learning disability	Adults	Mental health	HQ Costs	Total
Total	**4,912**	**2,256**	**1,324**	**850**	**515**	**128**	**9,984**
HQ costs	-	-	-	-	-	128	128
Area officers/senior managers	104	155	26	27	24	-	336
Care management/care assessment	279	354	58	78	95	-	863
Residential care	2,942	690	737	200	208	-	4,776
Non-residential care	1,541	952	487	382	169	-	3,531
Field social work	46	105	17	17	18	-	203
Other	-	-	-	147	-	-	147

In accordance with CIPFA guidance, a number of Support Management costs are reallocated to individual client groups. See General Notes Section

Contact: Brian Allen 020 7972 5595
brian allen@doh.gsi.gov.uk)

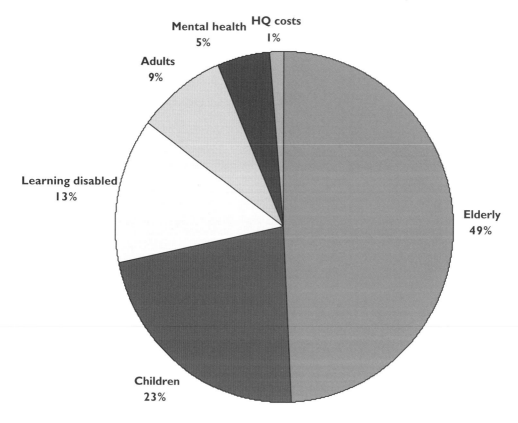

Personal social services gross expenditure by client group, 1997-98

- About half of gross expenditure was on provision for the elderly and nearly a quarter on provision for children.
- Central and Strategic costs account for only 1% of gross expenditure.
- Nearly a quarter of elderly gross expenditure was recouped through sales, fees and charges.

Tables A1, A2

The life tables on which these expectations are based use current death rates to describe the mortality levels for each year.

Each individual year shown is based on a three year period, so that for instance, 1996 represents 1995-97.

The 1997 data are provisional.

Tables A3, A4

Cause specific rates exclude neonatal deaths (deaths to infants under 28 days).

Figures represent the number of deaths registered in each year.

Table A7

Information on smokers is based on respondents who stated that they smoked at all nowadays.

Table A8

Regular smokers are respondents who stated that they smoked at least one cigarette a week; occasional smokers are respondents who stated that they smoked less than one cigarette a week.

Table A9

A unit is 8 grams by weight or 1cl/10ml by volume, of pure alcohol.

This is the amount contained in half a pint of ordinary strength beer or lager, a single pub measure of spirits (1/6 gill or 25 ml), a small glass of ordinary wine and a small pub measure of sherry or fortified wine.

Table A10

A person may report using several drugs, one of which is recorded as the "main" drug used and the rest as subsidiary drugs. This analysis is based on the main drug only.

These figures show users who presented to services for problem drug misuse for the first time or for the first time for six months. They do not give a complete picture of people receiving treatment.

Tables A11

The table reflects final numbers after correction (excluding original cases in port health authorities).

Tuberculosis data excludes chemoprophylaxis.

Meningococcal septicaemia are without meningitis.

Table A12

HIV/AIDS data correct as at end of March 1999, but cases particularly for recent years continue to be reported.

Table A13

Conceptions include those resulting in a maternity and those terminated by a legal abortion but exclude spontaneous abortions (miscarriages).

All ages conception rate is per 1,000 women aged 15-44.

Further information is available in the ONS annual publication "Conceptions in England and Wales".

Table A14

Perinatal mortality rate equals still births plus early neonatal deaths (up to 7 days) per 1,000 live and still births.

Infant mortality rate equals deaths up to 1 year per 1,000 live births.

Information about caesarean sections in 1992 to 1998 is for financial years commencing 1 April.

Further information is available in the Department of Health Statistical Bulletin: NHS maternity statistics, England: 1989-90 to 1994-95.

Collection of information about community maternity services started in 1988-89; information is for financial years commencing 1 April.

Table A15

Grounds as listed in Schedule 2 of the Abortion Regulations, 1968 (as amended by the Human Fertilisation & Embryology Act 1990) -

A Risk to life of woman.

B To prevent grave permanent injury to physical or mental health of woman.

C Risk of injury to physical or mental health of woman (pregnancy has not exceeded its 24th week).

D Risk of injury to physical or mental health of existing child(ren) (pregnancy has not exceeded its 24th week).

E Substantial risk of child being born seriously handicapped.

F In emergency - to save life of woman.

G In emergency - to prevent grave injury to physical or mental health of woman.

The full definition of statutory grounds appears in the introduction to the ONS annual publication "Abortion Statistics".

Table A16

Family Planning Clinic Activity includes data for Brook Advisory Centres.

Table B1

1. Principals, assistants and vocational dental practitioners at 30 September.

2. A principal is a general dental practitioner on a health authority/ family health services authority list.

3. Patients were first registered under the new dental contract in October 1990. Registrations built up until 1992 and were affected in subsequent years by improved checks on duplicates. Figures shown for 1998-99 are affected by the change to the registration period to 15 months for registrations starting from September 1996 onwards.

4. Adult patient continuing care registrations at 30 September.

5. Child patient capitation registrations at 30 September.

6. The figures are based on the Appropriation Account.

Table B2

The figures for examination and report from 1991-92 exclude full case assessments and treatment summaries.

Table B3

Figures for the number of practitioners relate to ophthalmic medical practitioners and optometrists who held contracts with HAs/FHSAs to carry out NHS sight tests as at 31 December. Those with more than one contract are counted only once.

From 1 April 1989, NHS sight tests were restricted to children aged under 16, students aged 16-18 in full time education, adults on low income, users of complex lenses and those with certain medical conditions or at risk of eye disease.

The Voucher Scheme was introduced on 1 July 1986. Under this scheme vouchers are issued to those who would previously have been eligible to receive NHS spectacles, to use towards buying their own choice of spectacles. People eligible for vouchers are children aged under 16, students aged 16-18 in full time education, adults on low income and users of complex lenses.

Table B4

Figures for "all prescriptions" cover all prescription items dispensed in the community in England, by community pharmacists and appliance contractors, dispensing doctors, and prescriptions submitted by prescribing doctors for items personally administered.

Figures for "exempt prescriptions" are based on a 1 in 20 sample of all prescription items submitted to the Prescription Pricing Authority by community pharmacists and appliance contractors only.

Exempt prescriptions cover the catagories elderly people, young people, war or MOD pensioners, Health Authority exemption certificates, NHS low Income Scheme Charge Remission (NHS LIS) and no charge contraceptives.

NHS LIS includes recipients of Family Credit, Income Support, Income based Job Seekers Allowance, Disability Working Allowance, and others who qualify on the grounds of low income.

The figures for "prescription items dispensed generically" and for "NIC of items dispensed generically" have been revised since the last publication. The statistical bulletin "Statistics of prescriptions dispensed in the community: England 1988 to 1998" explains the revisions. (Please note that further revisions to the dispensed generically figures shown in the bulletin have been made in this publication.)

Dressings and appliances have been excluded in calculating the percentages of drugs dispensed and prescribed generically.

The graph shows the percentages of the total number of all prescription items and the total net ingredient cost for the top six British National Formulary (BNF) chapters, in terms of net ingredient cost, for all prescriptions dispensed in the community in England in 1998. The figures show that drugs dispensed in the community for cardiovascular treatment accounted for the largest proportion of both total net ingredient cost (20 per cent) and total number of prescription items (20 per cent).

The net ingredient cost (NIC) is the basic cost of a drug. This cost does not take account of discounts, dispensing costs, fees or prescription charges income.

Table B5
Further information about community pharmacies is published in annual statistical bulletins.

Table B6
Collection of information about community nursing and cross-sector services started in 1988-89.

Table B7
Collection of information about cross-sector services started in 1988-89.

Table B8
Further information about cancer screening is published in annual statistical bulletins.

Table B9
Uptake figures in 1987-88 are percentage immunised by end of calendar year in which their second birthday falls.

BCG immunisation program was delayed in 1994-95 when resources were diverted to the national MR immunisation campaign.

Table B10
1. Each occasion on which a patient was in contact. The number of individuals will be smaller than this.

2. Includes people who did not require treatment or advice from the Community Dental Service.

3. Numbers of dental education patient contacts are no longer collected.

4. Number of episodes of care in which a patient received treatment or prevention of oral disease. The number of individuals will be smaller than this.

5. In some years Health Authorities have been unable to produce a breakdown of the total figures.

In these cases the total does not add up to the sum of the individual age groups.

Background information

The Community Dental Service (CDS) runs different programmes which are set up to check the oral health of the community.

These programmes are as follows:-

Screening programmes:- this is the process by which CDS covers a large population using simple tests to identify individuals who require dental care including counselling and advice.

Dental Health Education and Preventive programmes - this is the process by which sub-groups of the population are educated and motivated to improve dental behaviour.

The CDS is responsible for providing dental care to children, nursing and pregnant women, disabled people and any patient who would not otherwise receive treatment through the General Dental Service.

Table B11

The figures for 1987-88 are estimates based on discharges and deaths adjusted using 1988-89 data where information was collected for both discharges and deaths and finished consultant episodes.

Well babies are included only in the well babies and all specialties columns. The maternity sector includes delivery episodes and birth episodes not resulting in well babies.

Day case information for 1987-88 only collected at an all specialties level.

Tables B12, B13, B14, B15

Data are taken from the Hospital Episode Statistics (HES) system. This anonymised database contains detailed administrative and clinical information.

A finished consultant episode (FCE) is defined as a period of healthcare under one consultant in one hospital provider. If a patient is transferred to a different hospital provider or to a different consultant within the same hospital provider a new episode begins.

The figures do not reflect the number of individual patients treated, as one patient could have more than one episode of care within the data year.

The completeness of HES data has improved significantly since it was introduced in 1987-88. However, due to continued variation in data quality across providers, there is still a need to compensate for known shortfall, i.e grossing. Grossed figures provide better estimates and improve time series comparisons. The grossing methodology compensates for known shortfalls in the data, and is based largely on the KP70 counts of FCEs.

The national totals in table do not equate exactly to the figure in table B11, as the grossing factors used are based on KP70 data, but are not directly comparable with them.

The table is additionally "grossed for unknown/invalid clinical data", in order to provide best estimates year on year for diagnoses and operative procedures.

A new computer system was introduced for the processing of 1994-95 HES data which adopted a revised grossing methodology and applied improved validation procedures. For the sake of consistency back years have been re-processed on the new system thus introducing small revisions to previously published figures.

Data for 1996-97 and 1997-98 are provisional and largely ungrossed.

In Table B14, the figures for "Persons" include cases where sex is not known.

In Table B15, two of the procedures (QA3 and FB1) are similar to two of the Clinical Effectiveness Indicators (D & Cs for menorrhagia and wisdom teeth).

Table B16
Number of bed days in the year divided by the number of days in the year.

The return was revised in 1996-97 to specifically include the separate collection of beds in paediatric intensive care wards, and NHS managed beds in residential care. Several Trusts have reclassified learning disabilities beds as residential.

Table B17
The table shows the position in eight specialties. The specialties shown accounted for 88.1% of all patients waiting for elective admission at the end of June 1999.

Table B18
In 1994-95 "referral attendances" attendances became "first attendances" and "consultant initiated attendances" became "subsequent attendances". The change in definition may have a small effect on the figures for 1994-95 and 1995-96.

Table B19
The table shows the national position in ten specialties. The specialties shown account for almost three quarters of all first outpatient appointments following GP written referral in England.

Table B20
The emergency admissions through A&E standard was monitored from 1996-97.

Table B21
Occupied bed days are aggregated periods of time in days of a patients stay in a hospital or community bed. Community beds include nursing homes, residential care homes or group homes.

All figures stated in terms of 1998-99 definitions to ensure compatibility.

Table B22
Data on NHS facilities are derived from available bed day figures supplied by NHS trusts on form KH03. The data are converted to an annual average daily number by dividing the total number of available bed days in the year.

In 1996-97, information on residential care wards and homes managed directly by the NHS was collected separately for the first time. It is clear that in earlier years trusts included these beds on the return under other headings.

Data for 1996-97 and 1997-98 are not therefore directly comparable with earlier years.

The figures on places in nursing homes and residential care are as at 31 March in each year.

Table B23
Data on NHS facilities are derived from available bed day figures supplied by NHS trusts on form KH03. The data are converted to an annual average daily number by dividing the total number of available bed days in the year.

In 1996-97, information on residential care wards and homes managed directly by the NHS was collected separately for the first time. It is clear that in earlier years some trusts included these beds on the return under other headings.

Data for 1996-97 and 1997-98 are not therefore directly comparable with earlier years.

The figures on places in nursing homes and residential care are as at 31 March in each year.

In 1996-97 some residential homes that thad previously been classified as for elderly people were reclassified as being primarily for elderly mentally ill people. There is therefore a discontinuity in the data between 1995-96 and 1996-97.

Table C1

Source: Department of Health returns SSDA 903 and CLA 100.

Figures for 1999 are provisional.

Figures for children looked after exclude those who are looked after under an agreed series of short-term placements.

Table C2

Children may be registered under more than one of the categories of abuse shown; the sum of the categories therefore exceeds the total number of children on the register.

"Other" includes categories not recommended and cases where no category was provided.

Total figures include unborn children.

Table C3

Source: Department of Health returns SSDA 903 and CLA 100.

A commentary on this data, a fuller version of this table, and details of how to obtain our comprehensive statistical publication on looked-after children are available in a downloadable format at: http://www.doh.gov.uk/public/cla9798.htm.

Figures represent children who ceased to be looked after in the year, where "adopted" was given as the reason that care ceased.

Figures for looked after children in this table exclude children who were accommodated under an agreed series of short-term placements.

Period of care refers to a continuous period of being looked after, which may include more than one placement or legal status.

Table C4

Source: Department of Health returns SSDA 903 and CLA 100.

A commentary on this data, fuller versions of this table, and details of how to obtain our comprehensive statistical publication on looked-after children are available in a downloadable format at http://www.doh.gov.uk/public/cla9798.htm.

Only the latest occasion on which a child ceased to be looked after in the year has been counted.

Figures exclude children who were looked after under an agreed series of short term placements.

Table C5, C6

Information relates only to home help and home care services purchased or provided by local authorities. Services commissioned by the independent sector (i.e. voluntary or private) without local authority involvement are not covered.

Data are for a sample week each year in September or in October. Information for 1998 is provisional.

Contact hours are the total number of staff hours spent in contact with or directly serving the client(s).

Data are collected on households receiving services - a household may include more than one client.

Table C7

Figures are of residents who are supported financially, either wholly or in part, by local authorities.

Only supported residents in *staffed* residential and nursing care homes are included.

"Independent residential care" comprises voluntary and private residential care homes.

"Independent nursing care" comprises voluntary and private nursing care homes.

Client group figures (elderly, physically/sensorily disabled adults, etc.) for 1994 to 1997 relate to all residents supported in homes which are primarily for that particular client group, and may include people of other client types For 1998 the figures relate to the condition of the client (i.e. the main reason for the provision of care for that person).

Prior to the implementation of the Community Care reforms in April 1993, local authorities were not able to financially support people in independent nursing homes.

In 1994 figures for the elderly and physically/sensorily disabled client groups were not collected separately.

Table D1

A new non-medical staff group classification was introduced in 1995 known as "new occupation codes"; comparative figures are not available for earlier years.

Nursing, midwifery and health visiting staff excludes agency and learners.

Medical and dental staff excludes locums.

Other direct care staff includes scientific, therapeutic and techical staff, nursing, midwifery and health visiting learners and health care assistants.

Other non direct care staff includes ambulance staff and other support staff.

The Source for this data is: NHS Hospital and Community Health Services Non-Medical staff in England and Hospital, Public Health Medicine and Community Health Service Medical and Dentral Staff in England.

Table D3

Nursing, midwifery and health visiting staff excludes learners and agency.

Medical and dental staff excludes locums.

Other staff direct care staff includes scientific, therapeutic and technical staff, nursing, midwifery and health visiting learners and health care assistants.

Other non direct care staff includes ambulance staff and other support staff.

Table D4

Nursing, midwifery and health visiting staff exclude learners and agency.

Medical and dental staff excludes locums.

Other direct care staff includes scientific, therapeutic and technical staff, nursing, midwifery and health visiting learners and health care assistants.

Other non direct care staff includes ambulance staff and other support staff.

Figures should be treated with caution as they are based upon organisations reporting 90% or more valid ethnic codes for non-medical staff.

Table D7

1. Principals, assistants and vocational dental practitioners at 30 September.

2. A principal is a general dental practitioner on a health authority/family health services authority list.

3. Figures for the number of practitioners relate to ophthalmic medical practitioners and optometrists who held contracts with HAs/FHSAs to carry out NHS sight tests as at 31 December. Those with more than one contract are counted only once.

Table E3

The expenditure figures are derived from annual financial returns of health authorities & NHS trusts.

Figures are reported on an income and expenditure basis, reflecting the gross value of goods and services supplied and capital charges incurred.

The capital charge for health authorities is made up of the depreciation charge plus the interest charge.

The capital charge for NHS trusts is made up of the depreciation charge only. The interest charge is 6% of total net book value of capital assets employed.

General supplies and services comprise all contract hotel services including cleaning contracts, which were included within the "Premises and fixed plant" category in previous years.

All expenditure relating to "Transport and moveable plant" is now included under "Establishment".

All expenditure relating to "External contract staff" is now included under "Miscellaneous expenditure".

Salaries & Wages bullet point -

Over the period 1997-98 inflation, represented by the "headline" Retail Prices Index (RPI), rose by 4%, while the RPI excluding mortgage interest payments rose by 3%. Source: NHS Pay Advance Letters/Office for National Statistics.

Table E4

Data on Personal Social Services current expenditure are collated on return RO3, made annually to the Department of Environment, Transport and the Regions (DETR) by Local Authority Treasurers departments in England.

Table E5

The current expenditure form RO3 was extensively revised in 1994-95 to accord with CIPFA accounting guidelines in "Accounting for Social Services" which were introduced in England and Wales in April 1993(April 1994 in Scotland).

The client groups used are those in the CIPFA guidance and will generally reflect the primary cause for placement/service provided.

The term "children" is generally understood as including all children,including those with disabilities; and "elderly" will generally include all or most elderly people.

This section provides a list of the Department of Health's statistical publications.

Note that publications with references such as 1999/25 are Statistical Bulletins that contain summary information. Other publications, such as those with ISBN numbers, are usually more detailed. Most publications relate to England.

See the DH statistics website (www. doh.gov.uk/public/stats1.htm) for up to date information.

Statistical bulletins and most other publications are available from:
Department of Health
PO Box 777
London
SE1 6LX

Tel: 0541 555 455
Fax: 01623 724 524
e-mail: doh@prologistics.co.uk

Section A - Public Health

Indicators of the Nation's Health
*   The Health Survey for England
        Summary of Key Findings booklet available for 1994 survey onwards
        Health Survey for England 1991   ISBN 0 11 691532 3   £27.50
        Health Survey for England 1992   ISBN 0 11 691569 2   £27.50
        Health Survey for England 1993   ISBN 0 11 691614 1   £38.00
        Health Survey for England 1994   ISBN 0 11 321895 8   £40.00
        Health Survey for England 1995   ISBN 0 11 322021 9   £60.00
        Health Survey for England 1996   ISBN 0 11 322091 X   £60.00
        Health Survey for England 1997: The Health of Young People ISBN 0 11 322266 1   £70.00
*   National Surveys of NHS Patients: General Practice 1998   ISBN 1 84 182104 7   £10.00
*   Access to GPs and Clinical Services outside office hours, England 1999   ISBN 1 84 182105 5
*   Public Health Common Data Set (only available within the NHS)
*   The Prevalence of Back Pain in Great Britain in 1998   1999/18

Health Related Behaviour
*   Statistics from the Regional Drugs Misuse Databases
        for six months ending March 1998   1999/7
        for six months ending September 1998   1999/19
*   Statistics on alcohol: 1976 onwards   1999/24
*   Statistics on smoking: England, 1976 to 1996   1998/25
*   Sun Exposure: Adults' Behaviour and Knowledge 1997   1998/3

Morbidity
- Epidemiological Overviews

Asthma	ISBN 0 11 321897 4	£11.00
Coronary Heart Disease	ISBN 0 11 321667 X	£11.00
Stroke	ISBN 0 11 321668 8	£11.00
Health of Elderly People	ISBN 0 11 321485 5	£10.30
Elderly People Companion Papers	ISBN 0 11 321486 3	£6.00
Health related behaviour- an epidemiological overview	ISBN 0 11 321976 8	£13.99

Fertility
- NHS Maternity statistics: England 1989-1990 to 1994-1995   1997/28

Section B - Health Care
- The New NHS Performance Tables 1997-98

Primary and Community Care

General Ophthalmic Services
- General Ophthalmic Services Activity Statistics:
- April to September 1998
- General Ophthalmic Services Activity Statistics:
  October 1998 to March 1999 and year ending 31 March 1999
- NHS Optical Voucher Survey 1998
- Ophthalmic Statistics: England 1988-1989 to 1998-1999   1999/27
- Sight Tests Volume and Workforce Survey, 1996-97 (annual report)

Pharmaceutical Services
- Community pharmacies in England and Wales (six monthly)
  - 30 September 1998   1999/1
  - 31 March 1999   1999/20
- General Pharmaceutical Services in England and Wales:
  1990-91 to 1998-99   1999/29
- Prescription Cost Analysis: England 1998   ISBN 1 84182 045 8   £12.00
- Statistics of prescriptions dispensed in the community:
  1988 to 1998   1999/17

Community Health and Prevention
- Breast Screening Programme, England: 1997-98   1999/9
- Cervical Screening programme: England 1998-1999   1999/32
- Chiropody services 1998-99
- Clinical psychology services 1998-99
- District nurses activity 1997-98
- Learning disability nurses 1998-99
- Maternity services - midwife clinics and domiciliary visits 1998-99
- NHS Contraceptive Services, England 1998-99   1999/30

- NHS Immunisation Statistics, England 1998-99   1999/28
- Occupational therapy services 1998-99
- Professional Advice and Support Programmes 1997-1998 (formerly Health visitor activity)
- Psychiatric nurses activity 1998-99
- Physiotherapy services 1998-99
- Specialist care nursing 1998-99
- Speech and language therapy services 1998-99
- Wheelchairs and Artificial limbs, 1996-1997   ISBN 1 85839 796 0

Hospitals
- NHS Quarterly Review
- Private hospitals, homes and clinics registered under
  Section 23 of the Registered Homes Act 1984, England, 1997   1998/14
- Private hospitals, homes and clinics - England Regional Health
  Authority and Regional Office Areas registered under Section 23
  of the Registered Homes Act 1984, Vol 1   ISBN 1 85839 495 3   £7.00
- Private hospitals, homes and clinics - District Health Authority
  summarises registered under section 23 of the
- Registered Homes Act 1984, Vol 2   ISBN 1 85839 496 1   £11.00

Hospital Inpatient Activity
- Bed availability and occupancy, 1997-1998   ISBN 1 85839 956 4   £9.00
- Elective admissions and patients waiting: England at 31 March 1998   1998/20
- Hospital Episode Statistics
    Vol 1: Finished Consultant episodes by diagnosis and operative
    procedure; injury/poisoning by external causes
    Vol 2: Finished Consultant episodes administrative tables
    Vol 3: Finished Consultant episodes: waiting times
    CD-ROM: Hospital episode statistics, England 1995-96
- Hospital waiting list statistics: England
    Monthly
    Quarter ended 30 June 1999   ISBN 1 84182 067 9   £10.00
    Responsible population based Quarter ended 30 June 1999   ISBN 1 84182 068 7   £8.00
- Imaging and radio diagnostics, 1997-1998
- NHS Hospital activity statistics: England 1987-88 to 1997-98   1998/31
- Ordinary and day case admissions 1997-98   ISBN 1 85839 958 0   £7.00

Hospital Outpatient Activity
- NHS day care facilities in England: 1998-1999
- Outpatients and ward attenders 1997-98   £9.00
- Waiting times for first outpatient appointments: quarter ending
    31 December 1998   1999/4
    31 March 1999   1999/14
    30 June 1999   1999/21
    30 September 1999   1999/31

- Waiting times for first outpatient appointments in England:
  Detailed statistics: Quarter ended 30 September 1999   ISBN 1 84182 115 2   £11.00

Patient's Charter
- Ambulance Services, England: 1998-99   1999/16
- Handling complaints: monitoring the
  NHS complaints procedures, 1997-98   ISBN 1 85839 976 9   £6.00

Mental Health & Learning Disability
- Electro-Convulsive Therapy: Survey covering the period
  from January to March 1999   1999/22
- Inpatients formally detained in hospital under the
  Mental Health Act 1983 and other legislation,
  England 1988-1989 to 1998-1999   1999/25
- Inpatients formally detained in hospitals under the
  Health Act 1983 and other legislation: NHS trusts,
  high security hospitals and private facilities: 1997-98   ISBN 1 85839 995 5

Section C - Personal Social Services
- Key indicators of Local Authority Social Services
  graphical presentation package only on CD-ROM
  (Updated at least twice a year)
- Key Statistics of Personal Social Services for year
  ending 31 March 1998 and Budgets for 1998-99

Children
- Children accommodated in secure units,
  England and Wales year ending 31 March 1998   1999/6
- Children and Young People on Child Protection
  Registers year ending 31 March 1999   ISBN 1 84182 098 9   £8.00
- Children's homes at 31 March 1997 (trienniel)
- Children looked after by Local Authorities year
  ending 31 March 1998 (detailed statistics)   ISBN 1 84182 044 X   £13.00
- Children looked after in England, 1998-1999   1999/26
- Supervision Orders year ending 31 March 1998 :England   1999/3

Adults
- Annual statement under section 17 (2) of the
  Chronically Sick and Disabled Persons Act 1970:
- Separation of younger patients from older patients in hospitals
  Annual statement under Section 18 (3) of the
- Chronically Sick and Disabled Persons Act 1970, on
  handicapped persons in residential care in England and Wales

- Community Care Statistics: 1998 Day and Domiciliary
  Personal Social Services for Adults   1999/10
- Community care: Detailed statistics on Local Authority personal social services for adults.
- Community care statistics: Referrals, Assessments and
  Packages of care (RAP), England – Report of the first
  Dress Rehearsal, 1 January to 31 March 1999
- Community care statistics 1998 Residential
  Personal social services for adults   1998/37
- Residential Personal Social Services for adults. Detailed statistics
  on residential and nursing care homes and local authority
  supported residents 1998   £8.00
- Guardianship under the Mental Health Act 1983, England 1998
- People registered as deaf or hard of hearing, England 1998 (Triennial)
- Registered blind and partially sighted people year ending March 1997 (Triennial)
- Report under section 11 of the Disabled Persons (Services),
  Consultation and Representation) Act 1986 on the development
  of services for people with learning disabilities or mental illness in England

Section D - Workforce
- General Ophthalmic Services Workforce Statistics,
  England and Wales: 31 December 1998
- Hospital, Public Health Medicine and Community Health
  Service Medical and Dental Staff in England 1988 to 1999   1999/15
- NHS hospital and community health services
  non-medical staff in England: 1988-1998   1999/12
- NHS Hospital and community health services non-medical
  workforce census in England: 30 September 1998   ISBN 1 84182 072 5   £15.00
- Personal Social Services staff of Social services departments at
  30 September 1998   1999/8
- Statistics for General Medical Practitioners in England: 1988-1998   1999/13
- General and Personal Medical Services Statistics,
  England and Wales: 1 October 1998   ISBN 1 84182 046 6   £15.00

Section E - Expenditure
- Personal Social Services: A Historical Profile of Reported
  Current and Capital expenditure 1983-1984 to 1993-1994
- Personal Social Services current and capital expenditure in
  England: 1997-1998   1999/11

DH STATISTICAL CONTACTS

If you can't find what you need in a publication, please telephone:

Skipton House, 80 London Road, London SE1 6LH   **020 797 (followed by ext number)**

Family Health Services (Branch SD1)

General dental and community dental services	ext 25392
General pharmacy services	ext 25504
General ophthalmic services	ext 25507
Prescription analysis	ext 25515

Hospital and Community Health Services (Branch SD2)

Mental illness/handicap	ext 25546
Community and cross-sector services	ext 25524
Demographic statistics	ext 25562
Drug misuse	ext 25550
Legal status	ext 25546
Smoking and alcohol	ext 25551
Hospital inpatient activity	ext 25529

Personal Social Services and Surveys (Branch SD3)

Children's services	ext 25581
Adults' services	ext 25585
Staffing	ext 25595
Financial (revenue out-turn expenditure) data	ext 25595
Key indicators	ext 25599
Health Survey for England and other surveys	ext 25560/92

Quarry House, Quarry Hill, Leeds LS2 7UE   **0113 25 (followed by ext number)**

Workforce (Branch STATS(W))

NHS medical staff	ext 45892
NHS non-medical staff	ext 45744
General medical services	ext 45911

Waiting Lists (Branch FPA-PA)

Performance Indicators	ext 46425
Waiting lists	ext 45555
Hospital activity	ext 45522

NHS Expenditure (FPA-PX1)   ext 45356

Richmond House, 79 Whitehall, London SW1A 2NS   **020 7210 (followed by ext number)**

Personal Social Services financial statistics (RMF-DPSS5)

PSS budget data	ext 5140

DH STATISTICAL CONTACTS

Wellington House, 133-155 Waterloo Road,
London SE1 8UG

020 797 (followed by ext number)

Central Health Monitoring Unit
Our Healthier Nation target monitoring

ext 24648

The Health Literature Line

0800 555 777

We would be grateful if you would spend a few minutes filling in this questionnaire (preferably a photocopy so others can also comment) telling us what you think of this publication.

Your details

Name _____ Organisation _____

Position in
organisation _____

Address _____

_____

_____

e-mail address _____

HPSSS publication

Is this copy of HPSSS (delete as appropriate)   yours / your organisation's / a library's / other

What do you use the publication for?

data for specific topics ☐

data for a wide range of products ☐

indication of what data are available ☐

indication of how to get hold of information ☐

other ☐

Do you have any comments/suggestions on the current content? (please give details)

_____

_____

_____

_____

_____

_____

_____

Give details of tables you would like to see included in the future?

_____

_____

_____

_____

_____

_____

How much would you/your organisation be willing to pay for this publication? (delete as appropriate)   up to £10 / £10 - £20 / £20 - £30 / over £30

Internet

Do you have access to the internet?   yes ☐   no ☐

Do you know that a kept up-to-date throughout the year internet version of HPSSS exists?   yes ☐   no ☐

If yes, do you use the internet version of the publication?   yes ☐   no ☐

If yes, will you still want a copy of the paper version?   yes ☐   no ☐

DH statistical publications

Which of the following other DH statistical publications do you use?

	paper	internet	CD
statistical bulletins	☐	☐	
other, usually more detailed statistical publications	☐	☐	☐
statistical analysis/graphical products e.g. HES, KIGS			☐

Other statistical publications

Which of the following other government statistical publications do you use?

Health Statistics Quarterly	☐
Population Trends	☐
Social Trends	☐
Regional Trends	☐

Thank you for completing the questionnaire. Please return the completed form to;

Peter Steele
HPSSS Editor
Statistics Division
Department of Health
Room 459C Skipton House
80 London Road
London SE1 6LH

If we receive your form by the end of February 2000 we will be able to take your views into account in planning the future.